My Scotland

SPHERE

First published in Great Britain in 2019 by Sphere

A CIP catalogue record for this book
is available from the British Library.

ISBN 978-0-7515-7256-8

Designed by Sian Rance for D.R. ink
Printed and bound in China by C&C Offset Printing Co., Ltd.

Papers used by Sphere are from well-managed forests and other responsible sources.

Sphere
An imprint of
Little, Brown Book Group
Carmelite House
50 Victoria Embankment
London EC4Y 0DZ

An Hachette UK Company
www.hachette.co.uk

www.littlebrown.co.uk

My Scotland
Val McDermid

Photography by Alan McCredie

sphere

Acknowledgements

My parents and my grandfather instilled in me a love of the Scottish landscape and an appreciation of its social history. Without their influence, I suspect my books would be very different. If they existed at all.

But more specifically, for this book, Alan and I would like to thank those who went out of their way to help us:

Historic Environment Scotland, who gave us access to St Andrews Castle and Dryburgh Abbey; Delmonicas, Glasgow, who allowed Alan to photograph their interior; Police Scotland, who permitted Alan to photograph their HQ in Fife, Kirkcaldy Police Station and Gayfield Square Police Station; the Ship Inn, Limekilns, who opened the kitchen after hours to cook us a magnificent fish supper; and the Scottish Government for granting us access to the splendid chandelier in Bute House, the official residence of the First Minister.

We are grateful to our editorial team who have worked so hard to make this book look as splendid as it does. Thanks to Adam Strange, Lucy Malagoni and Zoe Gullen.

And finally, we'd like to thank our families – Jo and Cameron, Jenny, Eilidh and Joe – for their forbearance of our absences and for their love, support and good humour!

Contents

Foreword

'To awaken quite alone in a strange town is one of the pleasantest sensations in the world.' So said explorer and celebrated travel writer Freya Stark.

The true beauty and wonder of literature is that it allows us to feel this sensation every day from the safety and comfort of our own homes. For the price of a good book or, even better, with a library card in hand, we can traverse the globe. We can experience the sights, shapes, cultures and histories of villages, towns, cities and landscapes across our own country and far from home.

I have loved novels and the stories they tell for as long as I can remember. Learning to read opened, and holds open to this day, a world far behind my own ken.

And when I think of the books I have loved most, those that have made the biggest impact on me throughout my life, it is so often their places, real or imagined, more than their plots or even characters, that evoke in me the most intense feelings.

When I was a child, I always had my nose in a book (whenever time allows, the same is true today). I had a habit (sometimes, such as on the occasion of my fifth birthday party, to the irritation of my mum!) of squirrelling away with a book behind the couch or under the kitchen table. With hindsight, I suspect this was my way of blocking out the real word, all the better to lose myself in the imaginary one contained in the pages of whatever book I was reading.

Fictional places would take shape in my mind's eye with extraordinary detail. To this day, if I close my eyes, I can see with utter clarity my version of the Enchanted Forest, Kirrin Island, Narnia, Middle Earth, Treasure Island … and so many more of the imaginary landscapes of my childhood years.

I mentioned earlier that my reading habits sometimes irritated my mum. It occasionally annoys my husband that I will go to great lengths to avoid film adaptations of books that I love. The simple reason is that

I don't want my mind's eye image of their places – or indeed characters – to be supplanted. I remember as a child looking forward to the TV version of Enid Blyton's *The Famous Five*, only to find myself, a few minutes in, stomping around the house complaining that they'd got it all wrong.

The ability to create places in my mind is one of the many reasons I love reading novels. And not just fictional places. There's nothing quite like having somewhere you know intimately brought to life on the page. Crime fiction, a genre I love, will always have an added appeal for me if it is set in my home city, Glasgow – like parts of Val McDermid's Lindsay Gordon series, featured in this book. Instantly being able to place myself at the scene, knowing the nooks and crannies, perhaps sometimes taking issue with the descriptions, will give a story a whole new dimension of enjoyment – and, of course, it's the polar opposite of constructing, detail by detail, the picture of an imaginary landscape.

And then there's the wide-open window on the world, and the ever-ready time machine, that books provide. There are countless places across the globe – at various periods in history – that I have visited in literature long before I ever set foot in them in real life. Places like James Joyce's Dublin, John le Carré's Berlin, the New York of Truman Capote or J.D. Salinger, Victor Hugo's Paris and so many more. Probably my favourite novel of all time, Lewis Grassic Gibbon's *Sunset Song*, opened my eyes to a part of my own country that was barely known to my teenage self.

Then there are all places in the world that I have not yet visited – Chimamanda Ngozi Adichie's Nigeria or Elif Shafak's Turkey, for example – that I feel more than a passing familiarity with, thanks to the descriptive powers of a talented writer and a touch of my own imagination.

At the time of writing this, I am re-reading Muriel Spark's *The Mandelbaum Gate*, which takes the reader deep into 1960s Israel and Jordan – places that I've never set foot in but which are so richly illustrated on the page that I feel as if I've been there.

So it is that fascination with where stories happen that so excites me about this wonderful book – a book that makes place, location and setting the central characters in a compelling story about the author's country of birth, her life travels through it and the way in which its beauty, culture and architecture have helped inspire and shape her more than thirty best-selling novels.

Val McDermid is without doubt one of the best novelists of modern times. In my opinion, she is our nation's greatest living crime writer – and given Scotland's wealth of riches in this regard, that is a big statement. Her novels have it all for fans of the genre – murder mystery, psychological drama, police procedure, cutting-edge forensic science. Her plots are pacy and intricately crafted, and her characters complex, interesting, fully three-dimensional. But she is also a master when it comes to describing and bringing to life the places that her stories unfold in.

In *Broken Ground*, the remote Wester Ross setting is front and centre at the beginning and stays there throughout, almost becoming one of the key characters. Of course, the fact that this book ends in the drawing room of Bute House, the First Minister's official residence, gives it an added thrill for this reader – but more importantly, it gives others a peek into a building that sits at the heart of our nation's democratic story.

But the brilliance of Val's storytelling and character creation, how good she is at the what, why, how and who of fiction, can mean that the where is not always what immediately grabs our attention.

What is so great about this book is that enables Val to put a spotlight on the lurking, silent characters in her stories – the places in which they happen.

And when we have the chance to really focus on these places, we realise just how vivid and essential to her books they are.

On the day I am writing this, by sheer coincidence, the Wemyss Ancient Caves Society has an exhibition in the Scottish Parliament. When I stopped for a chat with the woman from the Society, she asked me if I knew much about the Caves. As I said that, yes, I knew a bit, it quickly occurred to me that much of what I know actually came from reading *A Darker Domain*, one of my favourites of Val's novels, which draws on the miners' strike of the 1980s.

Another of my favourites is *The Skeleton Road*, which features the magnificent Victorian Gothic building, until recently home to Donaldson's School for the Deaf.

On occasional childhood trips to Edinburgh, passing that building was a source of fascination to me. I would wonder about all the dark and exciting adventures that might have taken place within its walls.

I wondered, but the brilliant imagination of Val McDermid brought it to life and placed it at the centre of a gripping international crime story. That this book also takes us to a village in Croatia dealing with the legacy of the Balkan wars tells its own story about Val's range and relevance.

The places in many of Val's books make great settings for her plots – but they are more than that. Karen Pirie – the character of Val's that I love best, to the extent that I really wish she was real – takes nocturnal walks around Edinburgh as a way of coping with her grief-induced insomnia. Through these walks, Val doesn't just bring to life the parts of our capital city that the tourists don't always visit, she also allows the city to shape the life and emotions of her central character.

My Scotland brings all of this to the fore. It is a real joy to read – and a joy to look at. It makes you think about Val's books afresh – notice things that perhaps you didn't first time around and marvel at the sheer brilliance and complexity of her writing. And it takes us on a wonderful tour of Scotland, showcasing along the way the towns and cities, landscapes, architecture and curiosities that make us who we are.

Val's mastery of language and Alan McCredie's stunning photography have combined to create a work of true beauty.

Nicola Sturgeon
First Minister of Scotland

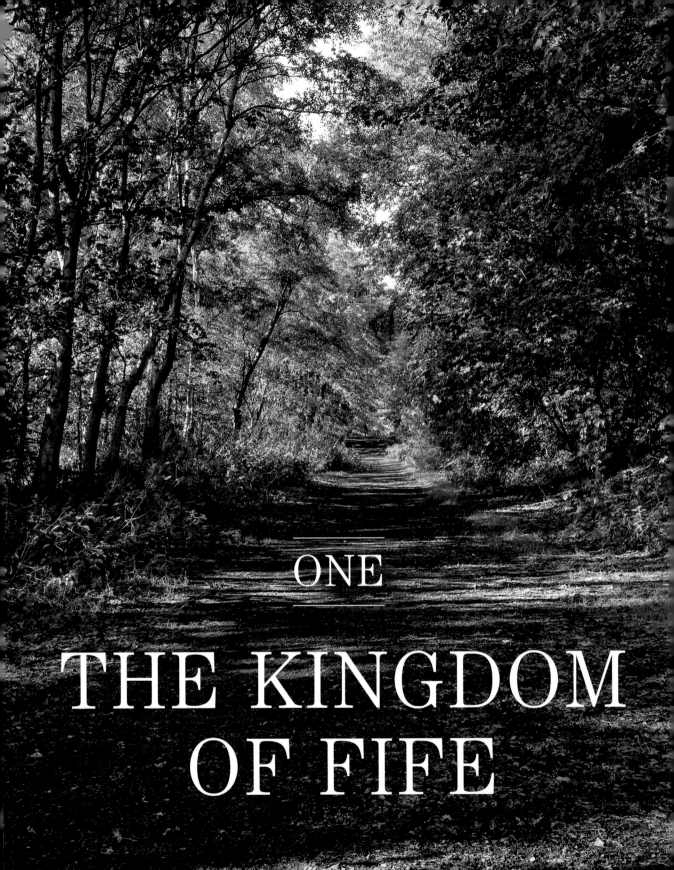

ONE

THE KINGDOM
OF FIFE

My parents never lived outside an eight-mile radius of where they were born, apart from a couple of years of wartime service. Lucky for me, then, that their stamping ground had so much to commend it. Thanks to them, I grew up between woods and beaches, hills and sea. But this wasn't simply some rural idyll. Kirkcaldy and East Wemyss, where I lived for the first seventeen years of my life, were also industrial landscapes. Dark red colliery winding gear and soot-blackened factories were never far from the horizon and their presence shaped my image of the world as much as nature did.

My fellow Scots are often scornful of the Kingdom of Fife, that peninsula on the East Coast where I grew up. They accuse us of being insular and parochial. It's a cheap laugh, from those who have no idea what Fife is really like.

It's true that Fife is distinct from its neighbours. It's surrounded on three sides by bodies of tidal water – the Firth of Forth, the Firth of Tay and the North Sea. Before we got the road bridges in the 1960s, going to Fife was a very deliberate choice, and often time-consuming. Once it became easier, some misguided civil servant in London thought the Kingdom should be split between Dundee to the north and Edinburgh to the south. The successful 'Fight For Fife' campaign that followed was my first political battle.

Kirkcaldy is famous for two things – linoleum and Adam Smith. The economist was born and raised there; and the town was the world capital of jute and linseed floor covering. When I was growing up, a miasma of linseed oil fumes hung over the town centre. It was also home to Seafield Colliery, the deepest pit in Scotland and one of the largest undersea coal mines in Europe.

Much more important, from my perspective, is the impressive neoclassical sandstone building that sits above the verdant Memorial Gardens and houses the library and art gallery. It was a by-product of linoleum – a gift from the Nairn family, the principal of a dozen

Johnny's Loan, Kirkcaldy.

manufacturers in the town. When I was six, my parents moved house to live across the road from the library and my fate was sealed.

My parents were working class, that cohort of respectable poor who believed that education was the way to a better life for their children. We couldn't afford books but when I was still a toddler my mother used to trail me half a mile across the council housing estate to the branch library to read me picture books. By the time we moved to the town centre, I could read by myself and I was already in thrall to stories.

The library became my home from home and I read my way round the shelves. Back then, you could only take out four books at a time and in Presbyterian Scotland, two of them had to be non-fiction. The line had to be held against the relentless encroachment of frivolity. But even on the non-fiction shelves, I managed to find stories. *Tarka the Otter*, *Norse Myths and Legends*, *Border Ballads and Tales* and plenty of others.

I love stories. My life has been book-ended and book-marked by hearing them, reading them and telling them. But from those early days in Kirkcaldy, the stories that have carved out the deepest impression in my memory and my heart have one common feature. *The Wind in the Willows*, *Treasure Island*, the *Chalet School* series, *I, Robot* – what they share is a sense of place. In my mind's eye, I can see where each of those stories unfolds.

I can't help wondering how much of that has to do with my childhood. For although my parents' lives were geographically circumscribed, they shared a restless desire to make the most of what lay around them. Every other Sunday, we would go for a run out in the car.

Sometimes there were definite destinations. Falkland, for the hill and the tearooms; St Andrews, for the historic ruins and the West Sands; Anstruther for the harbour and the fish suppers; Scotlandwell to watch the gliders; Milnathort for the ice cream.

But even better than those anticipated delights were the mystery tours on random roads. On a whim, my father would turn on to a previously untravelled road, just to see where it might take us. We explored back roads and undistinguished hamlets, discovered stunning views and standing stones, came across pretty houses and mysterious ruins. He had to make embarrassing three-point turns when a lane dead-ended in a muddy farmyard, tyres splashing through puddles, mad-eyed

sheepdogs snapping at our bumpers and deafening us with a demented cacophony of snarls, yelps and barking.

One afternoon, we found ourselves on a narrow road, climbing far more steeply than my father had anticipated. That would have been fine on a summer afternoon. But this was January and we were soon above the snowline on an unploughed road with nowhere to turn back. Of course we ended up in a ditch. We were completely unprepared. No food, no flask of coffee, no travelling rugs, no shovel. So we sang. (I learned everything from Cole Porter to murder ballads in the back of the car, but that's another story.)

We sang till we were getting on for hoarse and the last of the light was fading. And then the farmer crested the hill in his Land Rover on the way to feed the sheep. He pulled us out of the ditch and escorted us to the nearest main road. Just as well, really, or I might not be here to write this.

The Sunday drives weren't the only way I learned the anatomy of my home turf. When I was five, my father came home with a puppy, a Labrador retriever cross. One of our neighbours was a police dog handler,

Kirkcaldy Galleries, home of the Central Library.

so Bruce was properly trained. And he was my ticket to freedom. My parents knew if anyone attempted to lay hands on me, the dog would see them off. It was like having a chaperone who never told me what to do.

There were plenty of options for a child with an appetite for exploration and adventure. (Though it has to be said, most of the adventure took place in my head, as I recreated the stories I'd read while I walked, with myself in the starring role.) Up at the back of the town was Johnny's Loan, a track that cut through woodland and fields for miles. There were side paths that meandered through dense woods, eventually emerging in the overgrown grounds of Dunnikier House. It's a country house hotel now, but back then it was a decaying Georgian mansion whose parkland had been sold off years before for school playing fields, a golf course, a housing development and the town crematorium. The best bit was the dilapidated remains of a walled kitchen garden, the perfect setting for my imagination. More practically, it was a regular destination for me and my father because the soft fruit that had once been cultivated now ran wild. Currants, raspberries, goosegogs and crab apples filled our buckets and provided more jam than any family could reasonably consume.

Then there was the shore. Most coastal towns take pride in their seafront. The best houses are the ones with an uninterrupted view out to sea. And Kirkcaldy has a splendid view across the Forth to Edinburgh, with Arthur's Seat and the Pentland Hills in the distance. But for reasons unfathomable to me, most of the properties along the prom face inland. The advantage to a child was that I never felt overlooked or spied on when the tide was out and I threw sticks for the dog on the beach.

From the beach, there were two choices. West took us along the coast past the ropeworks and the sweet factory and the ruins of Seafield Tower, alongside the railway line all the way to Kinghorn.

But for me, east held more appeal. First there was the walk round the harbour basin and the harbour itself, where there were always boats and sometimes ships – fuel for the imagination of a child who'd read *Kidnapped* and Arthur Ransome.

Then there was the wide sweep of the bay beneath the ruins of Ravenscraig Castle, planned by James II of Scotland in the mid-fifteenth century as a gift to his wife. We'd learned Sir Walter Scott's ballad *Rosabelle* at school, and I still remember feeling astonishment that a proper poet had written a poem that was set in a place I actually knew. (Of course, Rosabelle died tragically on a dark and stormy night, but that was only to be expected, given the nature of most ballads.)

Beyond Ravenscraig the tide dictated the route. High tide meant climbing up past the ruined dovecote to the park and walking through the woods to Dysart harbour. Low tide offered the alternative route of the beach, scrambling over rocks and jumping over pools, which presented a different kind of narrative possibility. Imagine my excitement when I read John Buchan's *Prester John*, which opens on that very beach.

After Dysart harbour came the square bulk of St Serf's Tower, the pretty white cottages of the Pan Ha', and the disused salt pans. Then, blocking the way, the black slag of the pit bing – the spoil mound from the Frances Colliery. The mine was known locally as the Dubbie because it was always wet underground and dotted with puddles, or 'dubs' in the local dialect. At low tide, it was relatively easy to scramble round the base of the slag heap. It never crossed my mind that a pit bing could move and obliterate everything in its path.

What filled me with far more excitement and dread than the bing was The Man in the Rock – a statue of a man caged in by iron bars carved into the soft sandstone cliff. I've since heard it called *Bonivard the Prisoner* or *The Prisoner of Chillon*, inspired by a cleric, historian and libertine celebrated in a poem by Lord Byron. I don't know who sculpted the desperate prisoner or why he was installed in the rock face between Dysart and West Wemyss, but it terrified me and fascinated me in equal measure. Sadly, it's no longer there. Coastal erosion has spared modern generations from that sinister surprise.

Beyond West Wemyss the path winds along the coast beneath the grounds of Wemyss Castle. The coast here is riddled with defunct coal mines, their names a powerful reminder that before the National Coal Board was set up in 1947, coal mines were the personal fiefdoms of rich and powerful landowners. Around the Wemyss estate and its satellite villages are the remains of pits called Randolph, Victoria, Francis, Albert, Hugo, Isabella, Lady Emma, Michael – all named for members of the Wemyss family. They even had a private railway to carry coal from the pitheads to the rail network.

My grandfather was a miner. He worked in the Wemyss family pits for more than thirty years before they were taken over by the NCB. He and his friends talked often of the successive earls of Wemyss as heartless employers and worse landlords. My grandparents, who lived much of their married life in tied accommodation, had been married for over fifty years before they finally had a bathroom and running hot water. In 1970.

I took my petty revenge in *A Darker Domain*, a cold case novel set against the backdrop of the 1984 miners' strike. I effectively demolished Wemyss Castle and replaced it with the fictitious village of Newton of Wemyss, complete with a gastropub to add to the sum of human happiness. I suspect my grandfather and his buddies would have approved.

Halfway between West Wemyss and East Wemyss sits the Lady Rock. One side is almost vertical, the other a steep slope. Sometimes I'd go there with friends from East Wemyss. The challenge was to climb up

The Man in the Rock.

the rugged rock face, then, using one of the thick vinyl mats that used to wash up from the pit, toboggan down the slope without sustaining the kind of injury that would bring adult wrath down on us. Really, it's a miracle I'm still alive.

The rock looms large in my memory, but walking the Fife Coastal Path now, you'd be forgiven for missing it. The opposite to the coastal erosion that took the Man in the Rock is the accumulation of sand and gravel and coal spoil that has raised the level of the shore here, reducing the former impact of the Lady Rock. Beyond it are the remains of a small harbour – not much more than a pier with a few iron rings set into it. But I remember what it used to look like, and that became the setting for one of the most dramatic moments in *A Darker Domain*.

Now, walking the section of the Fife Coastal Path that runs from the Lady Rock to the Wemyss Caves, there is nothing to show that this part of the shore was dominated by the surface buildings and the two red steel frames of the headgear of the Michael Colliery where my grandfather worked. It was the largest coal mine in Scotland when it closed in 1967 after an underground fire. Three hundred and eleven men were working that night; the miners formed human chains, holding on to belts and hands, and led each other through fire and smoke to safety. Nine men didn't make it. It could have been so much worse, we all knew that. The collateral damage visited on the village of East Wemyss after the closure was the long tail of the tragedy itself.

But I remember what was up there before. The dirty white surface buildings sprawled across the headland for years after the disaster, a grubby memorial to nine lost lives and two and a half thousand lost jobs. The shuttered windows where weekly wage packets had been handed over; the shell of the most modern pit baths building in the country; the empty offices; the boarded-up canteen where my grandfather used to sneak me and my friends in for steamed pudding and custard; and the sealed entrances to the shafts where the cages delivered men from the surface to the coalface.

I don't remember why or how it came about, but my grandfather once took me down in the cage. I must have been five or six years old. I'd probably been driving him crazy with questions about what it was like down the pit. (I suspect his habit of educating me and the local children in the natural history of the woods and the shore spawned a lasting curiosity in me.)

I remember walking into the cage holding his hand. There were maybe half a dozen other miners there in their filthy pit-black working clothes, their black helmets with the lamps strapped to the front, tin boxes with their sandwiches hooked on their belts. The familiar smell of coal and stale sweat clung to them. I wasn't scared because I was with my grandfather.

I should have been scared because the drop of the cage was a terrifying plummet into darkness. It fell like a stone and I felt I'd left my stomach on the surface. No rollercoaster has ever held any fear for me after that.

I don't remember much about the mine itself apart from the heat and the stink. The mineral smell of coal dust and the human smells of men confined day and night in an airless underground tunnel formed the kind of miasma that I could still taste after we returned to the surface. Even after the visit to the canteen, it clung to the back of my throat.

The last stop on my coastal walk before I headed inland to my grandparents' home was the Wemyss Caves. But more of them later; they have their part to play.

This was the world of my childhood. This was the set dressing for my earliest stories. I learned to use the individual elements of my environment to make my tales more vivid, to feed my imagination. All these years later, I continue to use the same technique.

The vivid conjuring of cityscape or landscape as the backdrop to emotional or physical action is one of the most powerful tools the writer possesses to persuade the reader to sign up for the experience.

When it works, we're transported to another place and time. Raymond Chandler's Los Angeles, Charles Dickens' London or Margaret Atwood's Gilead become as real to us as the room or train carriage or coffee shop where we're reading. When we visit places for the first time, we feel a dislocating sense of familiarity because we already know Sara Paretsky's Chicago, Emily Brontë's Yorkshire moors or Arnaldur Indriðason's Reykjavik.

It lulls us into a sense of conviction. If the author is telling us the verifiable truth about the place, then we're inclined to believe everything else they're presenting to us even though we know deep down that it's all a fiction. So when I grew from reader to writer, I knew I'd be sustained by the places I knew best; that way I might be able to create believable worlds, whether real or imaginary.

In my experience, places fall into two broad categories – the ones that grab you by the throat and demand to be written about, and the others that sit waiting in the searchable database of the memory until you need precisely what they have to offer.

In this book, I'm going to introduce you to places that fall into both of these categories. This is a journey around my storybook Scotland – the locations that I've used in my books and stories. I hope you enjoy the trip.

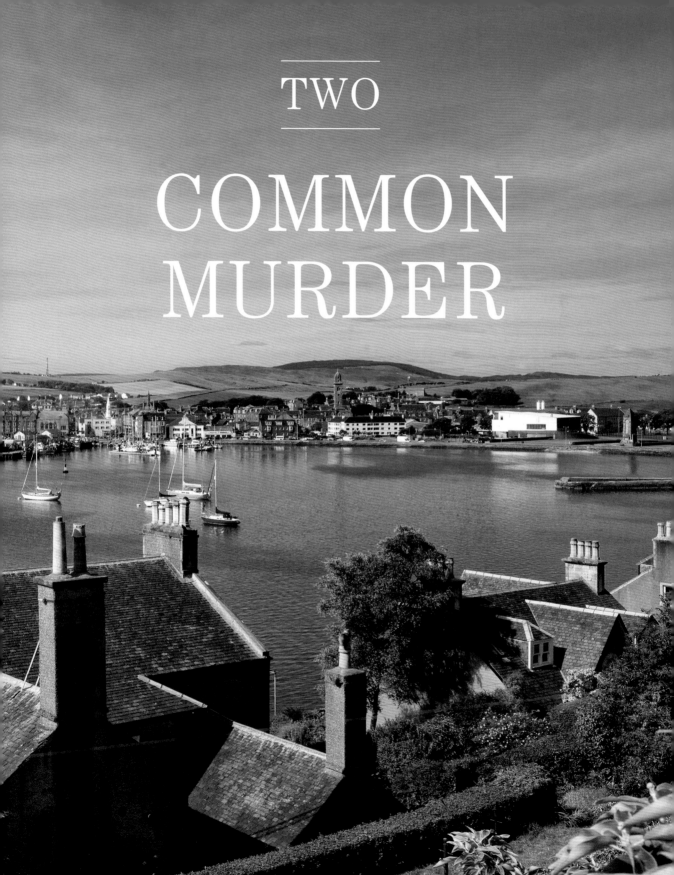

TWO

COMMON MURDER

By the time I started work on my first published novel, *Report for Murder*, I was living in exile. Well, that's what it felt like. I was working in the Manchester office of a national Sunday newspaper and living in Buxton in Derbyshire. It's the highest market town in England, surrounded by a bowl of hills and the dramatic scenery of the Peak District. Looking back at that choice now, I can't help feeling that some part of the reason I chose Buxton was that it was the nearest I could get to a sense of belonging. The hills, the woods, the stone-built houses, the caverns that burrowed into the limestone, and the moors all had a family resemblance to home. And in the winter, it got properly cold. With snow.

And although *Report for Murder* is mostly set in Derbyshire, I couldn't resist basing my protagonist, Scottish journalist Lindsay Gordon, north of the border. She's a freelance, living in Glasgow and selling stories wherever she can, which is what brings her down south on an assignment that swiftly turns into a murder investigation.

I'd spent two years working as a news journalist in Glasgow before I moved south and I gave Lindsay bits of my own experiences. I should say that while she has the trappings of my life – my nationality, occupation, sexuality and a flat very similar to mine! – she is very definitely not me. Our personalities are quite different and I certainly wouldn't hurtle heedlessly into danger the way she often does.

I'd gone to Glasgow to work on the *Daily Record*. I've often encountered a surprised reaction from people who didn't expect me to opt for a tabloid after gaining an Oxford degree in English Language and Literature. But once I'd settled on journalism as a job to tide me over till I could make a living writing fiction, working for a red-top had been my goal. The *Record* had been the paper of choice in our house and I believed that working people deserved newspapers that were informative as well as entertaining. I gave Lindsay my youthful idealism along with everything else.

I'd arrived in Glasgow with a degree of apprehension as well as excitement. Strange as it may seem, I'd previously spent as little time in Glasgow as I had in Oxford before I arrived to study there. About a day and a half, in other words.

Although only forty-five miles separate it from Edinburgh, the two cities are startlingly different. The poet Hugh MacDiarmid spoke of the Scottish character exemplifying an anti-syzygy – the yoking together of two opposing forces. On the one hand, the wildness of the Gaelic temperament: music, whisky, laughter, passion, lust and pleasure. On the other, the buttoned-up Presbyterian character: restraint, reserve, hypocrisy, seriousness and absolutely no hanky-panky outside marriage. The common view is that Glasgow and Edinburgh are the very embodiment of the anti-syzygy. Vers libre versus the villanelle, if you like.

What I knew of Glasgow before I arrived:
- My cousin, who had been to university there, said it rained twice a year. From September to April and from May to August.
- According to William McIlvanney's *Laidlaw*, it was a city of violence and hardship.
- Sectarianism was a brutal and ugly reality, as witnessed in the clashes between football fans whenever Celtic and Rangers played each other.
- Billy Connolly was the epitome of an extravagant and outrageous sense of humour that burned brightest among those with least to lose.

What I didn't know of Glasgow before I arrived:
- It's beautiful. It was the second city of empire and its streets and squares are studded with glamorous buildings. The long streets of tall sandstone tenements – even those still ingrained with generations of industrial pollution – have a presence that knocks spots off the brick terraces of other cities. What I also didn't know then was that the capital to build them came from slavery, sugar and tobacco. I know better now but it still doesn't diminish their impact.
- Its name means 'dear green place' in Gaelic, and there are more than ninety public parks and gardens in the city.

ABOVE: Billy Connolly mural in central Glasgow

PREVIOUS SPREAD: Campbeltown; Lindsay Gordon grew up somewhere like this.

- Everybody speaks to you in Glasgow. Everybody has an opinion and not a shred of reluctance about sharing it.

The great advantage about being a news journalist rather than a specialist is that you get to know a city very quickly. Every day brings another story; another street; another cast of characters. Glasgow was a daily adventure for me, and I was up for it.

It helped that, for the first time in my life, I had brass in pocket. A national newspaper hack's wages felt like riches beyond dreams of avarice after three years of university and two years of training. I could afford to enjoy the theatre, the live music, the restaurants and the nightlife. Not to mention exploring the dramatic landscapes around the city.

Being from the East Coast, I'd been led to believe none of this existed. Nobody ever mentioned the Citizens Theatre with its distinctive production style; the gloriously eclectic and eccentric Burrell Collection; the sprawling Necropolis filled with idiosyncratic memorials. And the countryside – Loch Lomond, the Campsie Fells, the Clyde coast: all on my doorstep.

It didn't take me long to feel at home in Glasgow.

Lindsay let me explain something of Glasgow to people whose knowledge of the city was as scant as mine had been. Here she is, returning home after a long day at work. She pours herself a whisky and settles down at her living room window.

… she gazed over the trees to the distant university tower which stabbed the skyline to her left. She always relished returning to her eyrie and loved the view that had nothing to do with the Glasgow of popular mythology; that hard, mean city composed of razor gangs and high-rise slums was not the city that most Glaswegians recognised as their home. Sure, there were bits of the city that were barely civilised. But for most people Glasgow now was a good place to live, a place with its own humour, its own pride.

Looking across Kelvingrove Park to Glasgow University from Park Circus.

But there were still sharp contrasts, nowhere more so than in the world of licensed premises. When I moved to Glasgow in the late 1970s, a popular pub we used to drink in didn't have a ladies' toilet. Lindsay's local in 1987 is marginally more civilised:

The floor was bare vinyl, the furnishings in the vast barn of a room were rickety in the extreme and had clearly never been much better. There was not another woman in sight apart from the calendar girl on the wall. But Lindsay walked confidently through, greeting several of the men at the counter … At the far end of the bar [she] went through a door into another world. The lounge bar was cosy, carpeted and comfortable.

In the second book in the series, *Common Murder*, Lindsay is based in London, working for a fictitious national newspaper. Newsgathering collides with her own past when she finds herself covering the women's peace camp at a US air base, a setting that drew heavily on my own experience of the Greenham Common protest. The uneasy overlap between Lindsay's professional responsibilities and her personal politics leads her into dark places, but the only time she makes it back to Scotland is towards the end of the book, when she returns to the fishing village in Argyll where she grew up.

The Invercross I invented drew on my occasional visits to Tarbert and Campbeltown when I lived in Glasgow. The heart of both is the harbour, where shops and houses cluster in picture-postcard formation. For Lindsay, it's a place that always conjures mixed emotions. But the 'spectacular views of the Argyllshire mountains and sea lochs' always touch her heart.

And I couldn't keep Lindsay away from Scotland for long. Researching *Final Edition*, the third in the series, gave me an excuse to spend weekends in Glasgow, for the city had undergone significant changes since I'd left. The garden festival in 1988 and the city's role as European City of Culture in 1990, the year I chose to set the book, had transformed the city physically and atmospherically. The city's slogan, 'Glasgow's Miles Better', summed up that civic pride. For at least some of its citizens, there had been a renaissance. It felt as if the city was consciously repositioning itself from an industrial manufacturing centre to a modern cultural hub.

OPPOSITE: Tarbert harbour.

ABOVE: Campbeltown Town Hall.

Final Edition celebrates the changes I saw in a city I'd come to love – the restoration of the Victorian Merchant City, the beginnings of a new gastropub culture, the claiming of the status of Scotland's most truly European city. As Lindsay says on the night of her return after nine months' exile in Italy:

'Nothing you've told me about this wine bar we're heading for sounds British to me. A place where writers, actors, lawyers and politicians go to drink good wine, eat serious food and put the world to rights sounds like café society in Paris or Vienna or Berlin, not bloody Glasgow … Every corner shop has got posters up advertising some cultural beanfeast. Everything from opera to open days, from puppets to psychodrama. I don't even recognise the streets any more. Where there used to be nice wee bakeries selling cream doughnuts and every other sort of cholesterol-packed traditional Scottish goody, there are wholefood cafés.'

Like Lindsay, I felt a bit of a stranger in a strange land. Having learned Glasgow from scratch, I had to start all over again and assimilate these changes, because this book draws on Lindsay's personal history so it had to be set there. In a way, it would have been easier to cut my losses and draw a line under Glasgow. But seeing the city through Lindsay's eyes forced me to look at it more closely than I might otherwise have done. I couldn't help falling in love with it all over again. But not entirely uncritically …

She turned into a narrow alleyway which opened out into a small courtyard with several staircases leading off it. Originally, these had been the semi-slum homes of the ill-paid clerks who had tended the fortunes of the Victorian merchants and shipping magnates who had once made the city great. Over the years, the properties had deteriorated, till they were precariously balanced on the edge of demolition. But in the nick of time, a new prosperity had arrived in Glasgow and the property developers had snapped up the almost derelict tenement slums and renovated them. Now there were luxury flats with steel doors and closed circuit video security systems where once there had been open staircases that rang with the sounds of too

many families crammed into too small a space. Lindsay surveyed the clean, sandblasted courtyard with an ironic smile.

We both wondered where those displaced families had gone. The answer of course was the less than lovely satellite council housing estates that had none of the city centre's glamour and precious little access to anything in the way of culture. They don't get much of a look-in during Lindsay's investigation but she does acknowledge them out of the corner of her eye; her politics are still very much to the fore in the way she moves through the landscape of her life.

And that's one of the things I'm conscious of in my own life. I love my country and its people, but it's not a sentimental attachment. I can be critical too. The great advantage of being a writer of fiction is that you can give your characters a wide range of views. So when I feel ambivalence or worse, I can explore that through other people's voices.

It's up to the reader to decide when it's me speaking …

Above: Hutcheson's Hall, Merchant City, Glasgow.

PREVIOUS SPREAD: Tower blocks in Springburn, Glasgow.

THREE

KILLING THE SHADOWS

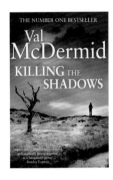

After *Final Edition*, I made a conscious decision to write a very different kind of book. It had been the new wave of American feminist private eye fiction that had propelled me into writing my own opening trilogy but I was eager to see whether I could make the PI novel work in the UK. One thing I knew was that all the US versions had urban backdrops that remained constant throughout the series. Since I was living in a city that was going through a particularly turbulent and interesting period, it seemed perverse not to take advantage of that. And so I took a deep breath and committed myself to writing about Manchester, both identifiably in the Kate Brannigan PI series and fictionalised (with grafts from other Northern cities) in the Tony Hill & Carol Jordan novels.

But I recognised that when I was writing about Scotland, living elsewhere was easier on me, and when I stopped doing that, I missed home all the more. There was no way I could shoehorn Scotland into the Kate Brannigan novels. Though I did give a bit-part in *Blue Genes* to a Glasgow punk band called Dan Druff and the Scabby-Heided Bairns.

Nor did it work for Tony and Carol – a different legal system made any crossover difficult to manage. I wanted to set a book in Scotland, but desire is never enough by itself.

For me, the story idea is the ignition point of a book. The characters are the drive chain that powers the engine. And usually the stories are site-specific – the location matters because it feels right for those lives and events that I'm going to be writing about. So I can't sit down and say, 'I'm going to write a book set in Scotland.' Or Serbia. Or Southampton. I'm always locked into a location that works for the story I'm trying to tell. There are some aspects of writing that don't leave a writer much wriggle room and for me, the world where the story exists is one of them.

Killing the Shadows was my second standalone novel. And it had to be set principally in London because the main elements of the plot demanded it. Someone is killing crime writers. The truly fiendish twist is that they're being murdered by methods of their own devising. The perpetrator tracks the victims down on their home turf then stalks them to find the chink in their lives that provides the opportunity for murder. It's a storyline that tends to make my fellow crime writers twitch, and look at me askance.

That stalking was the plot device that let me stage a couple of key elements in Scotland. And that in turn gave me the excuse to revisit those places. Because who knew what might have changed since I'd last been there? It's always the things you think you know that catch you out.

That happened to me with *The Grave Tattoo*. Back when I was a journalist, I'd searched the national records of births, marriages and deaths myself at St Catherine's House. It never occurred to me that the archives had been moved, so I confidently described St Catherine's House in the book. I was showered with letters and emails complaining about my inadequate research, for a few years previously the registers had been relocated to a completely different borough of London. You don't check something you're sure of precisely because you're sure of it.

My protagonist in *Killing the Shadows* is Dr Fiona Cameron, a geographic data analyst who sometimes places her profiling expertise at the disposal of the police. She's eventually invited to examine the cases of the dead writers, which takes her to Edinburgh, the home of the first victim. I let her stay in Channings Hotel, where I'd regularly been made welcome as a guest of the Edinburgh International Book Festival. And I gave her a room with a view:

> Through the smirr of rain, she could see the steely ribbon of the Firth of Forth. Over on her left, a vast looming Gothic pile with an intimidating spire dominated the streets spread below her. 'What's that building?' she asked the porter just as he was leaving.
>
> 'That's Fettes College,' he said. 'Where Tony Blair went.'
>
> It explained a lot, she thought.

ABOVE: Fettes College in Edinburgh.

PREVIOUS SPREAD: Loch Shin.

Because a sense of place is about more than description. It's about the responses of characters to their surroundings. So talking about place also includes politics, economics, romance, history, pain and many other matters.

There will be more about Edinburgh later, so for now, let's leave Fiona walking back to her hotel late at night.

> She was almost the only person on the streets. She turned on to the Dean Bridge, enjoying the spectacle of walking above tree-top level, with random blocks of light from the New Town tenements glowing pale yellow through the insubstantial mist.

Later, the story takes Fiona into the Highlands, to the eastern side of the watershed in the sprawling county of Sutherland. I was seventeen when I first experienced this part of the country. I was having an adventure in the summer between school and university. I was travelling across to the west coast on a Post Bus, which is exactly what it sounds like. It's a minibus run by Royal Mail that carries passengers and delivers letters and parcels along the way. I'd been lulled by the familiarity of gently rolling fields, so similar to the fertile heart of Fife. Then suddenly, everything changed. How Fiona tells it is how I experienced it too:

> Then she was driving along the narrow inlet of the Kyle of Sutherland, the dark water lined with heavy conifer forests, making somehow sinister the sunlit route into the wilderness that spread out ahead of her. As she turned up the River Shin towards Lairg, she could see she was entering the north-west Highlands proper, with sudden vistas opening ahead of rounded hills brown with heather, their rocky outcroppings grey and random. Scattered in the landscape were the ruined walls of croft houses, often just a pair of battered gable ends left standing. This was the landscape of the Highland Clearances, that brutal depopulation of the countryside where crofters had been driven off their land by rich landowners eager to make the easier money that came with rearing Cheviot sheep. Now the fragments of their homes were the only sign that this had been the starting point for the Highland diaspora that had colonized the British Empire …

Dean Village and the New Town at night, from the Dean Bridge.

Fiona, a keen walker, thought she was on familiar ground – 'She knew the springy feel of heather beneath her feet, the treacherous pull of peat hags, and the hard clatter of stratified rock beneath her boots.' It's a landscape that looks wide open, a place so bare and empty it could have no secrets. But that apparent candour disguises all sorts of surprises and hiding places. Traps and dangers too. Innocent-looking stretches of grass that hide treacherous peat bogs that will suck at your feet and set you sprawling; clouds of midges that will eat you alive if you stand still long enough; lochans that lurk in corries, invisible until you breast what barely feels like a rise in the moor. And sudden raging torrents of water that cut across what you thought was your path. Fiona was fortunate enough to find a bridge across a river gorge, the Allt a' Claon …

> Halfway across the bridge, Fiona slowed to a crawl and looked down fifty feet of craggy rock to the river's rough and tumble below. It was flowing fast through the channel it had cut itself, bursting into white foam as it hit the boulders that had fallen into its path. Cut off from the sparkle of sunlight by the high walls of the gorge, it gleamed the dark cloudy brown of unpolished amber.

It's the perfect wilderness for a set piece designed to set the reader's pulse racing faster than the red deer that occasionally flash across the moors. That first trip across Sutherland was unforgettable; even as a teenager, I was storing up memorable backdrops for my future career as a writer.

FOUR

THE LAST TEMPTATION

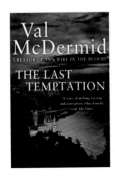

Clinical psychologist Dr Tony Hill and police detective Carol Jordan first appeared in *The Mermaids Singing*, working in the fictitious Northern English city of Bradfield. After the shocking denouement of their second outing in *The Wire in the Blood*, Tony traded his work at the sharp end of offender profiling for sanctuary in academe. He abandoned the North of England and took up a senior teaching post at St Andrews University, rented a cottage in the East Neuk fishing village of Cellardyke and even managed to find a girlfriend.

I moved him there because it was the only way I could think of to get a bit of Scotland into a novel whose events take place almost exclusively on mainland Europe. The waterways of Germany, Holland and France are at the heart of *The Last Temptation*, but I wanted the security of more familiar ground, at least to start with.

The East Neuk is the picture-postcard corner of Fife. The half-dozen settlements that dot the coastline owed their existence to the bountiful offshore fisheries with their apparently endless supply of haddock and, at the right season, the shoals of herring, those silver darlings celebrated in song. Fishing was a hard life and a dangerous one, even in coastal waters, and it fostered a sense of community as strong as any, with a raft of traditions and superstitions set in stone.

Now there is precious little fishing out of those sturdy stone harbours but the higgledy-piggledy huddle of fishermen's cottages that surround them in tightly packed narrow streets have been restored, repainted and refurbished and now exist as a magnet for holidaymakers, weekenders and commuters. And that's where I sent Tony Hill to recover his equilibrium.

Cellardyke blends seamlessly into its neighbour, Anstruther, home of the excellent Scottish Fisheries Museum. They look out across the Firth of Forth and beyond to the North Sea, the long low slump of the May Island bird sanctuary interrupting the horizon. The village takes its name from a couple of Scots dialect words – 'siller', meaning silver, and 'dyke', meaning a wall. So, the nets hung out to dry round the harbour walls glittering with fish scales were enough to give it a name. Less romantically, the harbour itself is referred to as Skinfast Haven. My father often called it that, and it always sounded to me as if it ought to belong in a Robert Louis Stevenson novel.

On our Sunday forays through Fife, we often ended up in one of the East Neuk villages, strolling along the coast, invariably finishing up with an ice cream. Fife has a significant population of Italians who arrived at the end of the nineteenth century bearing the twin blessings of ice cream and fish suppers. Fife is studded with award-winning chippies, many of them making their own ice cream to complement delights such as deep-fried Mars bars. Some even deep-fry the ice cream itself. It's no wonder Scotland is one of the leading nations of the world when it comes to heart disease and obesity …

But sometimes on our wanderings round the Neuk, we managed something denied to most visitors. We got past one of those forbidding wooden doors that lined the pavements, into the home of a genuine fishing family.

The people of the Neuk were clannish and tribal, cleaving to their own in matters of marriage. But somehow, my landlubber father's cousin James Carson had married into one of those tribes and become a fisherman. Occasionally we would stop by for a visit. From the outside, their house looked like any other cramped into those tight lanes. But inside was another story.

The kitchen was like an Aladdin's cave. Working-class homes in Fife in the early 1960s, homes like ours, seldom had fitted kitchens. They certainly never had gadgets like the Carsons' kitchen. There was a food processor on a breakfast bar. A blender that gleamed with glass and chrome. A pop-up toaster, even. I'd never seen anything like it. I could feel the waves of envy coming from my mother, a good plain cook and a first-class baker. I sat on a high stool at the counter and marvelled at what glories could be camouflaged behind such an unassuming façade.

ABOVE: George Street, Cellardyke.

PREVIOUS SPREAD: Cellardyke harbour.

I didn't give Tony a kitchen like that but I did give him a cottage with a view of the sea and a tiny garden with straggling plants struggling to survive in the face of the sharp salt winds. And when Carol tracked him down in a bid to tempt him back into harness, I had them meet in an off-season quayside pub in Pittenweem, the next village along the coast.

The barman looked up from his paper and gave her a quick smile. She glanced around, taking in the fishing nets draped from the ceiling, their brightly coloured glass floats dulled by years of cigarette smoke. Watercolours of East Neuk fishing harbours dotted the wood panelling of the walls. The only other customers appeared to be a couple of elderly men, their attention firmly on their game of dominoes. There was no sign of Tony.

He was still there at the start of *The Torment of Others*, but not for long. This was his swansong to the East Neuk.

From the top of Largo Law, the Firth of Forth lay before him, glittering in the late spring sunshine. He could see right across to Berwick Law, its volcanic cone the prehistoric twin to his own vantage point, separated now by miles of petrol blue sea. He checked off the landmarks: the blunt hump of the Bass Rock, the May Island like a basking whale, the distant blur of Edinburgh. They had a saying in this corner of Fife: 'If you can see the May Island, it's going to rain. If you can't see the May Island, it's already raining.' It didn't look like rain today. Only the odd smudge of cloud broke the blue, like soft streamers of aerated dough pulled from the middle of a morning roll. He was going to miss this when he moved on.

LEFT: Fishermen's cottages with traditional crow-stepped gables.

PREVIOUS SPREAD: Anstruther harbour.

FIVE

THE DISTANT ECHO

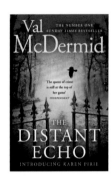

The Distant Echo is the novel that introduces Scottish cold case detective Karen Pirie in a minor but crucial role. As soon as the book started to take shape, I knew it had to be set in a prestigious university in a small town, ideally with a claustrophobic feel, and I knew the very one. Where else but St Andrews, in Fife? And so Karen Pirie ended up as a fellow Fifer.

Scotland's oldest university dates back to 1413 and it's been attracting students and academics from all over the world since then. Only about a third of its undergraduates are Scots; I've heard fellow Fifers quoting Rupert Brooke,

> 'That there's some corner of a foreign field
> That is for ever England.'

Nevertheless, I had school friends who'd chosen it, so I had my fair share of student nights out there. Not to mention the traditional morning-after route-march up the long stretch of the West Sands with the chill north-easterly wind blowing away the remnants of the night before. I had my first Chinese meal in St Andrews. My school debating team partner and I had made it through to the finals of a competition sponsored by the university and we were taken out to dinner before the debate. Remarkably, the restaurant is still there on Market Street. It looks like they're still serving the same menu as they did in 1971 …

So I knew enough about the town to realise it was the perfect place to set down four young men from Kirkcaldy who find themselves inadvertently suspect in a murder investigation that casts a long shadow over their futures. And because *The Distant Echo* has a split time frame – 1978 and 2003 – I was able in those earlier sections to draw heavily on my own teenage experiences and observations.

But although this is a small town, it has more than one focus. It's the home of golf, and the Royal and Ancient clubhouse is one of the town's landmarks. When we ended up in St Andrews on one of our family Sunday outings, although we'd park near the Old Course, we'd turn our backs on the golfers and walk along the Scores, the road that runs along the cliffs. University buildings sit between the road and the sea for part of the way, but they soon give way to the imposing ruins of the castle.

And it's the castle that provides the location for one of the most chilling episodes in the book. Among its notable features, the castle boasts the Bottle Dungeon. It is exactly as described – a dungeon in the shape of a bottle. The entrance is via a narrow neck that opens out into a wide circular chamber. There is no way out other than a rope let down from above. The first time I saw it as a child, it thrilled and chilled me in equal measure. Although I didn't know I was doing it at the time, I filed it away in the back of my mind where it lay dormant until I needed to inflict terror and suffering on one of my characters. The sturdy padlock that holds the protective iron grille firmly in place was no match for his assailants.

Beyond the castle and the cliffs that provide another dramatic scene in the novel are the cathedral ruins. It's in the atmospheric graveyard there, among the ancient headstones, that I placed the crucial encounter that ends in the Bottle Dungeon. When I began work on the book, I'd planned to make that graveyard the crime scene my unfortunate quartet of students stumbled on.

But that all changed because of a chance conversation. Because part of the book is set in 1978, I needed to soak up the historical ambience. What was happening in St Andrews? What films were being shown at the cinema? How much was a can of lager? The best source for that kind of information is almost always the local paper. I made an appointment to look through the bound archive of the *St Andrews Citizen* for 1978, and when I took a break from poring over the pages and making notes, I fell into conversation with the receptionist.

ABOVE: The entrance to the Bottle Dungeon.

PREVIOUS SPREAD: St Andrews Cathedral ruins and graveyard.

When she asked what I was up to, I explained I was researching a crime novel. 'Are you going to find a body in the Pictish cemetery?' she asked.

I had never heard of the Pictish cemetery, so I pressed for details. It's located on Hallow Hill – perfectly placed for an entirely reasonable shortcut back to student residences after a party across town. All that remains of the cemetery are groups of stubby stones arranged in the shape of the small coffins or kists used by the Picts for ceremonial burials. When I walked up there later that afternoon, I knew I'd found the perfect scene for an opening set-piece. So often, serendipity plays a crucial role in diverting the best-laid plans of writers.

It's not only glamorous St Andrews that features in *The Distant Echo*. This was the first book I'd set mostly in my native Fife, and my four central characters all came from Kirkcaldy. Their adolescent world was, broadly speaking, mine. Their New Year celebration was mine, too.

They crossed the road and walked down Wemyssfield, the short street that led to the town square. They had the confident stride of men on their home turf, a place so familiar that it conferred a kind of ownership. It was ten to twelve when they trotted down the wide, shallow steps that led to the paved area outside the Town House. There were already several groups of people passing bottles from hand to hand.

There was no official celebration in the square, but over recent years, groups of young people had taken to congregating

LEFT: The Pictish Cemetery on Hallow Hill.

PREVIOUS SPREAD: Bottle Dungeon, St Andrews Castle; Castle Cliffs.

there. It wasn't a particularly attractive place, mostly because the Town House looked like one of the less alluring products of Soviet architecture, its clock tower greened with verdigris. But it was the only open space in the town centre apart from the bus station, which was even more charmless. The square also boasted a Christmas tree and fairy lights, which made it marginally more festive than the bus station.

And their regular haunts were also mine. Where they stretch their legs is part of my frequent teenage walk from Kirkcaldy to Dysart and beyond. When I wrote this section, I could see every step in my mind's eye. I don't think I ever felt more exiled from my past than when I was writing this book.

The day before they were due to return to St Andrews, they met up in the Harbour Bar for a lunchtime pint. Flush with their Christmas earnings, Alex, Mondo and Weird would have been happy to make a session of it. But Ziggy talked them out into the day. It was crisp and clear, the sun watery in a pale blue sky. They walked through the harbour, cutting between the tall silos of the grain mill and out on to the west beach …

As they approached the castle, Alex peeled off and scrambled up the rocky outcropping that would be almost submerged at high tide. 'Tell me again, how much did he get?'

Mondo didn't even have to pause for thought. 'Magister David Boys, master mason, was paid by the order of Queen Mary of Gueldres, widow of James the Second of Scotland, the sum of six hundred pounds Scots for the building of a castle at Ravenscraig. Mind you, he had to pay for materials out of that.'

'Which wasn't cheap. In 1461, fourteen timber joists were felled from the banks of the River Allan then transported to Stirling at the cost of seven shillings. And one Andrew Balfour was then paid two pounds and ten shillings for cutting, planing and transporting these joists to Ravenscraig,' Ziggy recited [also from memory] …

[Alex] leaned back and looked up the cliff to the castle. 'I think the Sinclairs made it much prettier than it would have been if old Queen Mary hadn't kicked the bucket before it was finished.'

RIGHT: Abbotshall Church and Kirkcaldy Town House.

PREVIOUS SPREAD: Ravenscraig Castle, foreshore and high flats, Kirkcaldy.

'Pretty isn't what castles are for,' Weird said, joining them. 'They're supposed to be a refuge and a strength.'

Although *The Distant Echo* is set mostly in Fife, it also visits the two cities that sit opposite the peninsula on the far side of their estuaries – Edinburgh, across the Forth, and Dundee, across the Tay. I created a fictitious Dundee University forensic chemist and sited his fictitious lab in the Old Fleming Gymnasium building. These days, when I need advice on any aspect of forensic chemistry, I turn to the very real Dundee University professor Niamh Nic Daéid. Whose lab, spookily, is in the Old Fleming Gymnasium …

Sometimes life imitates art in the most peculiar ways.

The Forth Railway Bridge from below; my great-grandfather was a riveter in its construction.

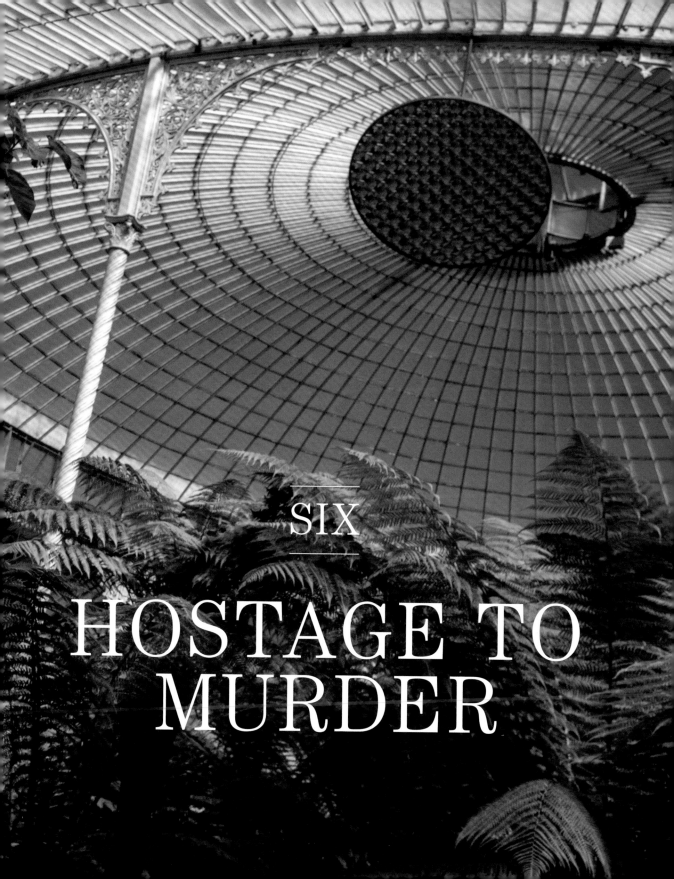

SIX

HOSTAGE TO MURDER

It turned out that even after the fifth book in what was supposed to be a trilogy, I couldn't leave Lindsay Gordon alone. And part of what made her irresistible was that I could inhabit Scotland again at her side. Just as Lindsay had come home from California to Glasgow, so I was able to join her, at least in my imagination, and revisit my old stamping grounds.

The book opens in the Botanic Gardens in Glasgow's West End, one of the city's most impressive parks. When I first moved to Glasgow to take up a job in the *Daily Record* newsroom, I rented a flat across the River Kelvin from the Botanics. It had huge rooms with high ceilings and the only heating came from a woefully inadequate two-bar electric fire. I was twenty-two years old and desperately trying to write but my flat was so cold and damp I couldn't work there.

So I used to take my pen and notebook across the bridge to the steamy warmth of Kibble Palace, the sprawling glasshouse at the heart of the gardens. I sat on a bench, occasionally dripped on by the condensation, attempting to write a novel. In the long wastes of the night shift when nothing much was happening, I'd type up what I'd written, revising as I went.

So when I needed a spot where Lindsay might reasonably have the sort of minor running accident that might require the help and support of a passing Samaritan, I thought of the steep path from the gardens down to the footbridge across the river. Her rescuer, fellow journalist Rory McLaren, takes her back to her flat. It's a few doors down from my rented one, but the interior is that of the one I later bought, round the corner in Clouston Street.

> Rory pulled open the gate that led out from the river bank on to the quiet backwater of Botanic Crescent. [She] keyed a number into the security door of a red sandstone tenement and ushered Lindsay into a spotless tiled close. They made their way up one flight of worn stone stairs, then Rory unlocked the tall double doors that led into

her first-floor flat. 'Excuse the mess,' she said, leading the way into the big dining kitchen at the back of the flat.

There was no false modesty behind Rory's words. It was, as she had said, a mess. A cat sprawled on a kitchen worktop by the window, while another lay curled on one of several piles of newspapers and magazines stacked on the floor. The tinfoil containers from the previous night's curry sat on another worktop alongside three empty bottles of Becks, while the sink was piled with dirty plates and mugs. Lindsay grinned. 'Live alone, do you?'

When I worked in Glasgow at the end of the 1970s, there was virtually no visible gay community. But by 2003, when *Hostage to Murder* was published, the picture was very different. There were bars and clubs where gay men and lesbians could meet and socialise, mostly around Glassford Street in the heart of the Merchant City. I'd created Lindsay because there were no visible images of lesbian life when I was growing up in Scotland, no name for what I felt, no templates for a life I could lead that expressed my heart. By the time I got to the sixth book, reality, books

Kibble Palace glasshouse and the Botanic Gardens, Glasgow.

and the wider culture had caught up. The next generation of teenagers who knew instinctively they were different would find themselves represented.

So too the places where they could meet. Around the turn of the millennium, one of those places was Café Delmonica (now simply Delmonicas) in Virginia Street. It became one of my regular haunts when I returned to Glasgow, handy for meeting friends who worked in the city centre. So when I needed a base for freelance journalist Rory, it sprang immediately to mind and earned a new incarnation.

> Café Virginia was suffering its daily identity crisis in the hiatus between the afterwork drinkers and the evening players. The music had shifted into more hardcore dance, making conversation more difficult, and there was a strange mixture of outfits on display, from business suits to teeshirts that clung to nipples and exposed midriffs.
>
> The quietest place in the bar was the corner booth where Rory McLaren ran her business and held court. Nobody else ever sat in the booth, mostly because of the foot-high scarlet neon sign that said, *RESERVED*. Rory had wanted it to say *GONNAE FUCK OFF?* but Mary the bar manager had vetoed it on the grounds that it would be too big for the table.

But there was also room in *Hostage to Murder* for the residential streets of the West End, an enclave of tall Victorian sandstone tenements colonised by academics, journalists, TV presenters, and students crammed into multiple occupancy flats. There's one street in particular, just round the corner from the old BBC building on Queen Margaret Drive, where almost everybody I ever met in Glasgow had perched at one time or another in a shared flat.

These tenements are imposing. Some are black with pollution, others have been sandblasted to reveal pale yellow or dark terracotta

Delmonicas in Virginia Street, the model for Café Virginia.

stone pierced by high windows. Blank street doors flanked by rows of doorbells open on to common closes, often decorated to waist height with beautiful glazed tiles – 'wally closes', as they're known locally. Inside, stone stairs wind upwards to the upper flats. When I worked in newspapers, the resigned maxim was, 'top floor, far door'. Somehow, this was always where the best stories lurked.

These were the streets I borrowed for *Hostage to Murder*. They hadn't changed much in the twenty-odd years since I lived there. And all these years later, they remain the same. The slum tenements of the south side were largely demolished in the 1960s. It was said at the time that they were beyond refurbishment. Thank goodness the developers only managed to get their hands on a few pockets of the West End.

A typical tenement corner in Hyndland in Glasgow's West End.

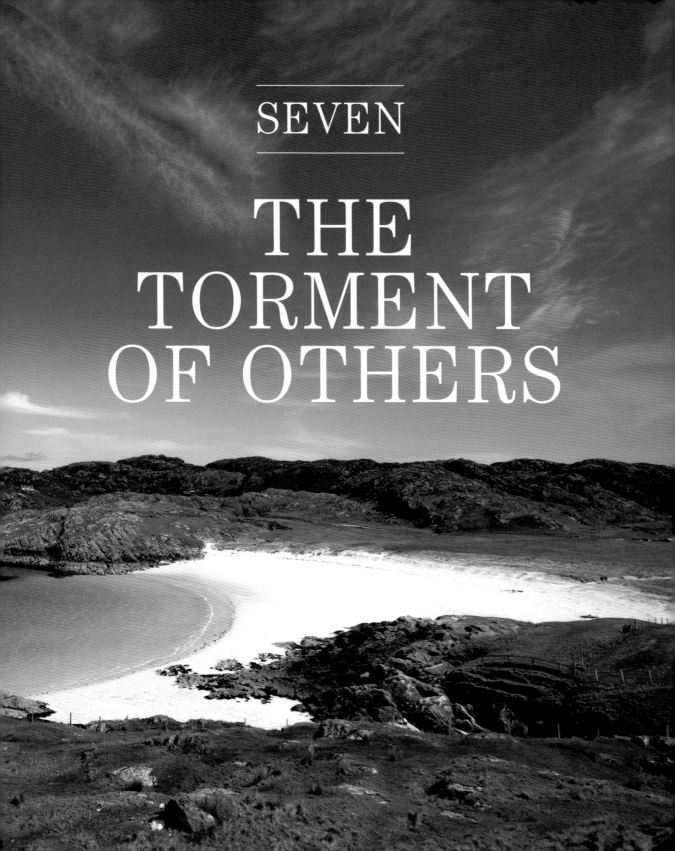

SEVEN

THE TORMENT OF OTHERS

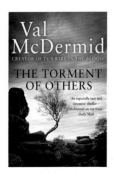

The Torment of Others, like almost all of the Tony Hill & Carol Jordan series, is set predominantly in the North of England. But as well as the dramatic scenery of the White Peak that I had come to love, it features a pivotal scene in a part of Scotland that has a very special place in my heart.

Sometimes writers evoke a place so powerfully we have to go and see it for ourselves. People make a living running literary tours, showing readers round the streets and alleys, the pubs and cafés where their literary heroes hang out. For me, the poetry of Norman MacCaig was an irresistible magnet that drew me true north to the Assynt region of Sutherland and its distinctive scenery. Assynt is a labyrinth of freshwater lochans, wild and desolate moorland, ancient rocks, and mountains that rise as singletons, each with a unique profile. And around the fringe, a spectacularly jagged coastline bitten into by strands and coves of pale gold sand. MacCaig wrote deeply moving metaphysical poetry about Assynt that laid claim to my heart in my teens. It still does.

I went there on a kind of pilgrimage the summer before I left Scotland for Oxford. I'd been working as a waitress in the Station Hotel in Kirkcaldy, saving money for my journeys north and south. Silver service waitressing was, I knew, a transferable skill and so it proved. I avoided depleting my savings by doing casual shifts at the Culag Hotel in Lochinver. In the bar there, Duncan, a seventy-two-year-old trawler skipper, proposed marriage on several occasions, some of them when he was sober.

In spite of his occasional gifts of lobsters and turbot, I was more interested in the Assynt landscape and I spent most of my nights at the Youth Hostel in nearby Achmelvich, making temporary alliances with other visitors as eager to get out in the hills as I was. I remember that summer in a golden glow of stories and song, seascapes and summits.

Achmelvich itself is a cluster of cottages; a Youth Hostel; a breathtakingly beautiful white sand beach; and, these days, a caravan site. The headland beyond the caravan site is a promontory of boggy

machair and weather-worn rocks splashed with the coloured lichens that give Harris tweed its distinctive shades. The sheep keep the grass trimmed and at first glance it looks like any one of thousands of similar outcroppings on the west coast and the Hebridean islands.

But the promontory at Achmelvich hides a remarkable surprise. Out on the rocks, perched on the side of a narrow inlet with a shingle beach the size of a rowing boat, is the Hermit's Castle. It's easy to miss; it's built of rough-cast concrete whose mix incorporates shells and grit from the beach below and it blends in perfectly with the shades around it. What catches the attention is sudden straight lines in a rounded landscape.

On closer inspection, it reveals itself as a cunningly designed bolthole, just big enough for one. There is no door; the entrance curves round like a snail shell to keep the wind out. There's a fireplace with an external chimney like a periscope, the right-angled bend facing away from the prevailing wind to prevent the smoke being blown back down. There's a concrete bed platform. The light comes from small square holes that once held glass bricks, long since vandalised.

There is, of course, a story. I've tried without success to verify the details, but it goes something like this.

ABOVE: Achmelvich Point with Hermit's Castle.

PREVIOUS SPREAD: Achmelvich Bay, Sutherland.

Back in the early 1950s, an architect from Norwich arrived in Assynt. It's said he was recovering from some sort of breakdown. He camped out on the point, travelling in and out in an open boat with an outboard motor. He had as little to do with the locals as he possibly could, and over a period of months, he built the Hermit's Castle. It must have been back-breaking work, carrying bags of cement up that steep, narrow climb from the beach; building wooden frames to pour the concrete into; mixing cement by hand. All that time on his own, without even a fresh water supply close at hand.

The story ends thus: he finished the construction, spent one night inside then left and never returned.

That summer, I often sat out on the promontory by the castle, watching the late evening sunsets splashing colour across the sky, backlighting the Isle of Lewis across the Minch, imagining the architect seeing that same view.

It was inevitable that I would write about it eventually. And so it became the setting for a fateful encounter in *The Torment of Others*.

He'd reached Achmelvich in the early evening, at the end of a single-track road that cut high above the slender finger of a sea loch. The occasional tree he'd passed had been bent double, a marker to indicate the force and direction of the prevailing wind.

The place was hardly worth giving a name to, he thought. There was the youth hostel, closed for the winter, and a handful of low cottages hunched along a spine of rock that stretched out into the sea. Only one of the cottages was showing a light. He wondered if he should ask for directions, but figured it couldn't be that hard to find this Hermit's Castle.

He'd been wrong, of course. He'd spent the best part of an hour clambering over rocks in the wrong shoes, stumbling on loose stones, nearly tumbling headlong into the sea at one point. When he'd finally found it, he'd almost walked straight past it.

Exhausted, cold and bruised, he shone his torch over the tiny concrete structure. It was nestled in a gap in the rocks, a grey box scarcely seven feet high with a small chimney curved over the roof like a tail. There was a doorway but no door. It led to a narrow passage that curved round, apparently designed to keep out the wind and the rain. It gave on to a tiny cell, barely six feet across. Along one side was a concrete shelf the size and shape of a single bed. Opposite was an open hearth. And that was it. Nowhere to hide, nowhere to do anything much. He couldn't imagine spending a day there, never mind a year.

That wasn't enough tribute for me to pay, however. Years later, I returned to the Hermit's Castle for a short story called 'Ancient and Modern'.

Then we crested a shoulder of the hillside and both stopped in our tracks. Ahead of us, on the edge of the cliff above a steep-banked inlet in the promontory was something so unexpected I wondered if I was hallucinating it. But a quick glance at Alan's face told me he could see it too.

A miniature fortress, geometric concrete shapes apparently growing out of the rock, topped with what looked like a periscope facing out to sea. There were small square holes in the concrete walls, blank eyes that my imagination filled with gun barrels pointing our way. It was completely incongruous, straight lines against the irregular humps and bumps and treacherous slopes of the rocks.

The story formed part of the *Bloody Scotland* anthology, a collection commissioned by Historic Environment Scotland, in which a dozen crime writers imagine terrible things taking place in the historically significant buildings of our choice.

Not just my Scotland, but other writers' too.

EIGHT

STRANDED

I don't write many short stories. I find them slippery and difficult and I often give up in despair then discover years later that they can be resurrected as a useful subplot in a novel. But over the years, I've managed a couple of dozen and many of them were collected in *Stranded*. The first British and US editions have one unique distinction – I took the photographs for the covers. Both were of boats literally stranded at low tide and beyond in the Aln estuary in Northumberland, just over the border with England. I chose those two vessels in particular because the one on the left has the barely visible remains of a Kirkcaldy registration dating from when it was a working fishing boat, and the other has a scabby Scottish flag, the Saltire, painted at the stern. I chose the title because of its ambiguity: strands of stories; the idea of stories weaving around each other to form a kind of rope; and because even as close to Scotland as North Northumberland, I still felt stranded on the wrong bank of the Tweed.

One of the stories in the collection – 'The Writing on the Wall' – owes its entire existence to an accident of location. In the early 1990s I was invited to take part in an evening of readings and discussion at the University of Glasgow with my fellow crime writer Liza Cody. At the time, we were both writing novels with female private eye protagonists, so we were regular public partners in crime.

The historic heart of the university is an elaborate Victorian Gothic confection built around a tower that dominates the skyline west of the city centre. From a distance it looks like an artistic child's version of a rocket ship bound for the stars. The original pale yellow sandstone has been blackened by years of industrial pollution. Rumour has it the stone can't be cleaned because it's only the compacted soot that's holding the building together. The tower is flanked by a pair of grand quadrangles which clearly state the intellectual aspirations of the university.

I'd lived less than a mile away when I worked in Glasgow, but I'd never made it inside the university precincts. Even though I was used to the

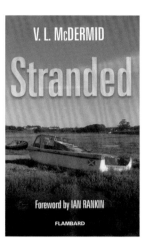

imposing architecture of Oxford, I found these buildings forbidding. But of course, the Gothic is predicated on us always allowing ourselves to be drawn into the lonely graveyard alone at midnight, and so I accepted the invitation to talk about my work within the confines of the university.

A helpful student directed us to the ladies' toilets before we went on stage. Time may have gilded my memory, for when I shared my recollection with my partner, who is a professor at Glasgow, it matched nowhere that presently exists. But my encounter took place more than twenty years ago, and the dead hand of modernisation is felt nowhere more keenly than in toilet facilities.

What I remember is a lot of dark wood panelling and heavy wooden doors. But the walls of the cubicles were painted some pale neutral colour. And on the wall of the stall I walked into was a terrible gift. There, in various hands and inks, was a tale of fear and pain. It started thus:

> I've never written anything on a toilet wall before but I don't know what else to do. Please help me. My boyfriend is violent towards me. He hits me and I don't know where to turn.

Other voices had joined the conversation, which straggled much of the way down the wall. One suggested kicking him where it hurts. Another told her to get out, that men only batter with our consent. Others offered more constructive solutions – ask friends for help; leave him; seek counselling. But it didn't end there. Those other voices began

PREVIOUS SPREAD:
Stranded beyond the reach of the sea on Scotland's east coast.

arguing with each other, then the original poster spoke of counselling. The messages extended down the wall then into a second column. It was harrowing but also compelling.

Graham Greene famously said 'there is a splinter of ice in the heart of a writer' that kicks in and allows us a dispassionate distance in moments of extremity. And I did feel a shocked compassion for a woman so desperate she'd turned to the anonymity of a toilet wall for advice.

But the ice kicked in and I copied the wall. Afterwards, with the distance of time and space, I crafted it into a short story with a darkly ambiguous ending. I still feel a twinge of guilt for exploiting that woman's pain. But there was nothing I could do to help her except to write a story that exposed the pain and shame of domestic violence.

LEFT: The River Kelvin walkway near the Botanic Gardens.

PREVIOUS SPREAD: Glasgow University East Quad.

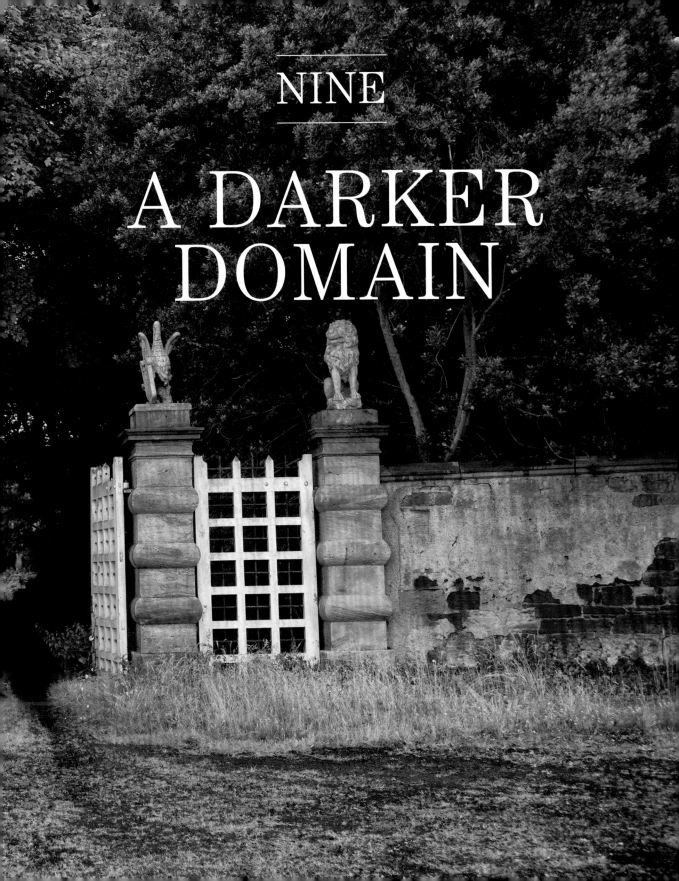

NINE

A DARKER DOMAIN

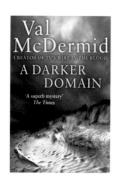

Just as *The Distant Echo* drew on some elements of my coming of age in Fife, so *A Darker Domain* is inspired by the landscapes of my childhood. The original cover was, as with *Stranded*, a photograph I took myself of the entrance to the Well Cave at East Wemyss. The Wemyss Caves play a crucial role in the book and the inspiration for that was the hours I spent exploring and playing in them as a child.

When I read Enid Blyton's *Five Run Away Together*, where the Famous Five set up camp in a cave on Kirrin Island, I was singularly unimpressed. Just one cave? In East Wemyss, we had half a dozen. The sea hollowed them out of the soft sandstone rock thousands of years ago, and they supported human occupation for much of that time. The walls of the caves are a treasure trove of carvings, some from the Bronze Age. Most significantly, the Wemyss Caves contain the highest concentration of Pictish carvings in Britain, dating back fifteen hundred years.

But we didn't care about that. What mattered to us was that we had a brilliant playground right on our doorsteps. What made it even better were the signs that warned us of danger, the placards saying, 'No Entry', and the possibility of being trapped by a particularly high tide. The caves gave us a jumping-off point for endless stories and adventures. We were pirates, we were cave dwellers, we were kings and queens holding court, we were outlaws on the run, we were secret agents.

Walking east from the village, first up is the Court Cave. King James V of Scotland allegedly liked to disguise himself as a commoner and mix with his subjects. According to local legend, he and a select band of his friends were carousing in the cave with a band of gypsies when things got out of hand. As they often will when drink is taken … To save himself, James had to reveal his true identity, and the scene of his embarrassment became known, in the traditional Fife spirit of ironic disregard for rank, as the Court Cave.

In more recent and more verifiable memory, my grandfather told me the Court Cave had long been the venue for the miners' favourite

RIGHT: The entrance to the Court Cave, East Wemyss foreshore.

PREVIOUS SPREAD: The gates leading to the Wemyss Castle estate near East Wemyss.

gambling game, pitch and toss. The rules were simple. A coin was set down as the target and everyone pitched their own coin at it. The man whose coin ended up nearest won the right to toss all the coins in the game. He got to keep all the coins that landed heads up. And then off-course betting became legal, and pitch and toss lost its charm.

We played there in the summer when there was long and bright daylight, for the Court Cave, its roof supported by brick pillars, wasn't the lightest of the caves and needed all the help it could get. There were side passages for hiding in, just right for leaping out at the unsuspecting. Their screams echoed beautifully in the high cathedral ceiling of the main cave.

But in winter, we moved along to the Doo Cave next door. It gets its name from the Scots version of 'dove' and the nesting holes that line the walls of the cave are a relic of the Middle Ages, when pigeons were bred here for meat to see the locals through the winter. The advantage of the Doo Cave in the darker months was that the pigeonholes were perfect for placing the candles we managed to get our hands on. The flickering light and the soft rushing of the sea over the shingle beach created the perfect atmosphere for telling the kind of spooky stories that thrilled the older kids and made the little ones cry. It was, I suppose, a kind of apprenticeship.

The other impressive aspect of the Doo Cave is the colours. The base shade is the familiar red sandstone of this part of the coast. But the combination of the sea air and the mineral traces in the rock have produced shades of green and grey, slashed with jagged patches and stripes of

The entrance to the Doo Cave.

white and black. By candlelight, it's an ever-shifting theatrical backdrop. All the better to spook you with.

We didn't bother much with the other caves, except to dare each other to crawl into the tight spaces where the cliff descended to meet the walls. We also spent a lot of time and torch batteries hunting for the supposed secret passage that led from the caves to the ruins of Macduff Castle on the headland above. I turned the myth into a kind of truth in my children's' picture book, *My Granny Is a Pirate*, using the idea to provide pirate Granny with an escape route from the beach to her cottage. (Not to mention a sweet spot for an ambush …)

When I started thinking about *A Darker Domain*, I knew from the start that I had the perfect site for a body dump. The momentous miners' strike of 1984 is the cold case backdrop to the story, and it's set just as specifically in place as it is in time. A man goes missing back in 1984. Local opinion brands him a strikebreaker, too ashamed or afraid to come back after the end of hostilities. And then a student archaeological field trip to the Wemyss Caves makes an unexpected discovery. Detective Inspector Karen Pirie, who leads the Historic Cases Unit in Fife, has her own memories of the locale:

Karen knew the caves that ran back from the shore deep into the sandstone cliffs between East Wemyss and Buckhaven. She'd played in them a few times as a child, oblivious to their historical significance as a major Pictish site. The local kids had treated them as indoor play areas, which was one of the reasons why the Preservation Society had been set up. Now there were railings closing off the deeper and more dangerous sections of the cave network and amateur historians and archaeologists had preserved them as a playground for adults.

She turned back towards the car park, looking along the seashore to the striated red sandstone bluff that marked the start of the string of deep caves huddled along the base of the cliff. In her memory, they were quite separate from the village, but now a row of houses butted right up against the outside edge of the Court Cave. And there were information boards for the tourists, telling them about the caves' five thousand year history of habitation. The Picts had lived there. The Scots had used them as smithies and glassworks. The back wall of

LEFT: The remains of the quay by the Lady's Rock, between East and West Wemyss.

PREVIOUS SPREAD: The pigeon holes in the wall of the Doo Cave.

The former HQ of Fife
Police in Glenrothes,
where Karen Pirie
began her career in
cold cases.

the Doo Cave was pocked with dozens of literal pigeonholes. And all of them had been used by the locals for purposes as diverse as clandestine political meetings, family picnics on rainy days and romantic trysts. Karen had never dropped her knickers there, but she knew girls who had and thought none the worse of them for it.

But her own experience doesn't prepare her for what lies within. I invented an extra cave – the Thane's Cave – and gave it a significant roof fall in 1985. But this is crime fiction, and nothing is ever as it seems, as forensic anthropologist Dr River Wilde explains to Karen and her colleague, Detective Sergeant Phil Parhatka.

River led the way to where the rock fall had blocked the passage leading back into the rock. Almost all of the boulders and small stones had been shifted, leaving a narrow opening. She played a powerful torch over the remaining rubble, showing that the actual fall was only about four feet deep. 'We were surprised to find how shallow this fall was. We would have expected it to go back twenty feet or more. That made me suspicious right from the word go.'

'What do you mean?' Phil asked.

'I'm not a geologist. But as I understand it from my colleagues in Earth Sciences, it takes a lot of pressure for a natural cave-in to happen. When they were mining underground around here, it produced a lot of stress in the rocks above, so you would get big fractures and falls. It's that scale of geological pressure that causes roof falls in old caves like this. They've been here for eight thousand years. They don't just collapse for no reason at all. But when they do go, it's like pulling the keystone out of a bridge. And you get a big fall.' As she spoke, River kept moving the torch beam around, showing that the roof was surprisingly sound on either side of the fall. 'On the other hand, if you know what you're doing, a small explosive charge will create a controlled fall that only affects a relatively small area.' She raised her eyebrows at Karen. 'The kind of thing that's done down mines all the time.'

'You're saying this fall was created deliberately?' Karen said.

'You'd need an expert to give you a definitive yes or no, but based on what little I do know, I would say it looks that way to me.' She swung round and shone the torch at a section of the cave wall about five feet above the ground. There was a roughly conical hole in the rock, black streaks staining the red sandstone. 'That looks like a shot hole to me,' River said.

'Shit,' Karen said. 'What now?'

'Well, when I saw this, I thought we needed to step very carefully once we'd cleared a path through. So I put on the J-suit and went through by myself. There's maybe three metres of passageway, then it opens out into quite a big chamber. Maybe five metres by four metres.' River sighed. 'It's going to be a bastard to process.'

'And there's a reason to process it?' Phil asked.

'Oh yes. There's a reason.' She shone the torch at their feet. 'You can see the floor's just packed earth. Just inside the chamber, on the left, the earth is loose. It had been tramped down, but I could see it was different in texture from the rest of the floor. I set up some lights and a camera and started moving soil.' River's voice had become cool and distant. 'I didn't have to go down far. About six inches down, I found a skull. I haven't moved it. I wanted you to see it in situ before we do anything further.'

You'll never look at a sea cave in quite the same way again.

Places speak to us for all sorts of reasons. There's a gatehouse on the Wemyss estate, about halfway along the main road from Coaltown of Wemyss to East Wemyss. It sits at an angle to the main road, next to tall gates that are a heavy lattice of wooden beams. They resemble a medieval portcullis, but rather than rising vertically, they open like a traditional gate. They had originally been painted white but they're always scabby and unloved in my memory. The gatehouse too looked unprepossessing – not intrinsically, but rather because it seemed uncared for. There was something about it that always made me think of Grimm's fairy tales. It was the sort of place I could imagine a wicked witch or a deranged woodcutter living.

I thought that was a pity. Even as a child, I could see it was potentially an attractive cottage in a great location. OK, there was a main road at the front, but the back led straight to the best kind of mixed woodland. Bluebells in spring, the smell of leaf mould in summer, fresh leaves to scuff through in winter. And only a fifteen-minute walk to the shore, if that. I'd have loved to live there.

And so I rescued it from my shabby memory. I gave it a complete makeover and presented it to Catriona MacLennan Grant, an artist in glass, the daughter of a rich man who had renounced her wealth for her art, and a single mother.

Sometimes, making stuff up is about making things better.

The gatehouse of the Wemyss Castle estate; a typical miners' row in the Wemyss villages, happily renovated.

TEN

TRICK OF
THE DARK

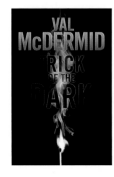

Trick of the Dark is my Oxford novel. But by far the most dramatic scene in the book takes place on the side of a mountain on Skye.

I was never a climber. My attempts at scaling rock during that summer in Assynt were an abject failure. I was better at falling off than staying on the simplest vertical face. That didn't stop me loving the hills, though. In Scotland, you can make it to the top of almost all of the highest mountains without anything more demanding than a bit of a scramble, so my inability to emulate my climbing friends didn't feel an insurmountable loss. I admired their skill and strength; I enjoyed watching them and listening to them talk about their conquests. I even read about the obsessive pleasures of mountaineering, from Andrew Greig's poetry to Chris Bonington's *I Chose to Climb*. Years later, reading Joe Simpson's *Touching the Void* planted a seed that took root in this book.

I first visited Skye in my late teens, joining my cousin, her husband and her in-laws for part of their summer walking holiday. The scenery was spectacular – the melodramatic profiles of the Cuillin ridges, the beauty of the ragged coastline, the ever-changing skies. But there were definite downsides, notably the ravenous midges, whose bites drove us mad with their incessant itching. These days, thanks to Edinburgh University researchers, Smidge spray has eased that problem.

Sgurr Alasdair is the highest mountain in the Black Cuillin range and also the tallest in the UK outside the mainland. It's a Munro – one of the 282 Scottish peaks that tower more than 3000 feet above sea level. At the very top is the Inaccessible Pinnacle, a tiny summit that offers astonishing views on a clear day. The In Pinn is the reason Sgurr Alasdair is the only Munro that requires climbing skills to complete. Like the rest of the Black Cuillin, it's made of gabbro, a rock that provides great grip, even in the wet.

So when I wanted to stage a climbing tragedy, my mind went straight to Sgurr Alasdair. Although I'd never made the full ascent, I had walked up the glen to the base of the mountain and hiked the lower slopes. Even

RIGHT: The Inn Pinn summit of Sgurr Alasdair from the end of Glen Brittle.

PREVIOUS SPREAD: Glen Brittle and Sgurr Alasdair, happed in mist.

on a fine day, it's a demanding walk. In winter, when snow and ice add their impact to the challenge, it's obvious why many climbers come here to practise for Alpine climbing. The changeable Scottish weather adds another layer to the difficulties, something which I was happy to exploit for the purposes of my story. Only a fool would fail to respect this climb. But even skill and respect may not be enough to survive it.

We had headlamps on, and even under the thin crust of snow there was no possibility of missing the start of the footpath, a wide depression running along the side of sheep pens. We could hear the rushing water of the Allt Coire na Banachdich, and before long we reached the wooden bridge that crosses the stream, which was a black-and-white torrent in the dawn light.

I wished we'd been able to leave later, because it was still too dark to appreciate the grandeur of the Eas Mor waterfalls tumbling down into the gorge. I remembered the guide book I'd bought the first time I visited Skye. 'On Skye,' it announced, 'it rains 323 days out of 365. Never mind. Think how lovely it makes the waterfalls.' Kathy wasn't impressed, not least because the occasional flurry of sleet was buffeting us in the face as we carried on up the rough path, past impressive buttresses and gullies that looked as challenging as anything I'd ever climbed. By the time it was fully light, we were surrounded by astonishing views – great crags, sensational shapes and contours, a jagged skyline, all streaked white with snow and glittering with ice.

When we first caught sight of the In Pinn it was a bit of a let-down. From that distance, it looks insignificant, a canine tooth a bit longer than the incisors and premolars around it. But as we scrambled and traversed, crossing bealachs – the Gaelic word for mountain pass – and scree slopes, the scale of what we were going to attempt gradually dawned on us. And it was daunting.

The pinnacle itself is an obelisk of gabbro, an imposing fin of rock that stretches 50 metres upwards from a small plateau just below the main summit of Sgurr Dearg. It doesn't sound much, but once you start the climb, there's a 1000-metre plummet to the valley floor on one side. If you can look at that without feeling vertigo, you've got a stronger stomach than most climbers.

We were quiet as we put on our harnesses and roped up in preparation for the climb. The rope is the symbol of the bond between climbing partners. Its practical purpose is to minimise the risk from dangers that the individual climber would struggle to handle alone. No matter how high your levels of skill, experience and physical ability, it's always psychologically easier to be attached to somebody else when you're struggling for the next handhold on a sheer slippery slab of rock.

The east route up the In Pinn was described by the Victorian climbers who first conquered it as a ridge less than a foot wide, 'with an overhanging and infinite drop on one side, and steeper and further on the other'. They weren't exaggerating. Technically, it's only a 'Moderate' climb in terms of the skills you need to be able to accomplish the ascent. But a glance to either side at any time during the ascent can make your bowels turn to water and your stomach flip. And in terms of the consequences if you get it wrong, it's totally unforgiving.

We set off up a short, steep but easy pitch, the perfect confidence-builder for what was to come. And so we began the next pitch, a section of rock that rewarded slow and steady progress. We'd built up a rhythm with hands and feet, moving with confidence, trusting the rock and trusting each other. At the halfway point, we stopped briefly on a ledge. But there was no shelter from the biting wind so we set off again almost immediately. The first few moves were tricky and I had to get my ice axes out, but then the route appeared as obvious as a flight of stairs.

But what a flight of stairs! Imagine crawling up a fifty-foot set of uneven steps with a sheer drop on either side. Now think about doing it on ice. Now think about doing it on ice with someone throwing handfuls of stinging snow in your face. For by now, our worst fear had come to pass. It was snowing. Not just the odd flurry, but great flakes that covered my eyes and filled my mouth and nose, hurled at me by the harsh wind. Kathy was only a few feet ahead of me yet I could barely see her.

When the change came, it came without warning. The rope jerked so suddenly and so hard it nearly pulled me straight off the mountain.

If I hadn't been wearing spiked crampons on my boots, I'd have been ripped straight off the icy surface to the valley below. As it was, I was yanked sideways so that the top half of my body was twisted across the ridge. The pain was instant and excruciating. My instinct was to grab the rope, to try to shift some of the weight that was pulling me on to the edge of the ridge so hard I could scarcely breathe. It took an agonisingly long time, but at last I managed to straighten myself enough to be able to catch my breath and try to work out what had happened.

The one thing that was clear as soon as I started thinking rather than reacting was that Kathy had come off the mountain.

But is our narrator reliable or not? Accident or murder? You'll have to read the book to find out …

Here's a footnote about Skye that sheds some light on what ends up on book jackets. Although I think of my novels as primarily urban in their settings, my UK publisher likes to use brooding landscapes on my covers. A few years ago, I did an event on Skye, promoting *Splinter the Silence*. The cover features a rustic triple-arched stone bridge over a torrent of water running through moorland, mountains in the background. When they saw the cover, my audience grew excited. They recognised the image – Sligachan Bridge on Skye. Someone raised a hand. Was this book set on Skye?

Regretful, I shook my head. 'No, it's set in the North of England and Devon. There isn't even a bridge in it. But the Art Department liked the picture.'

Thankfully, their disappointment didn't stop them buying the book.

Sligachan Bridge on Skye.

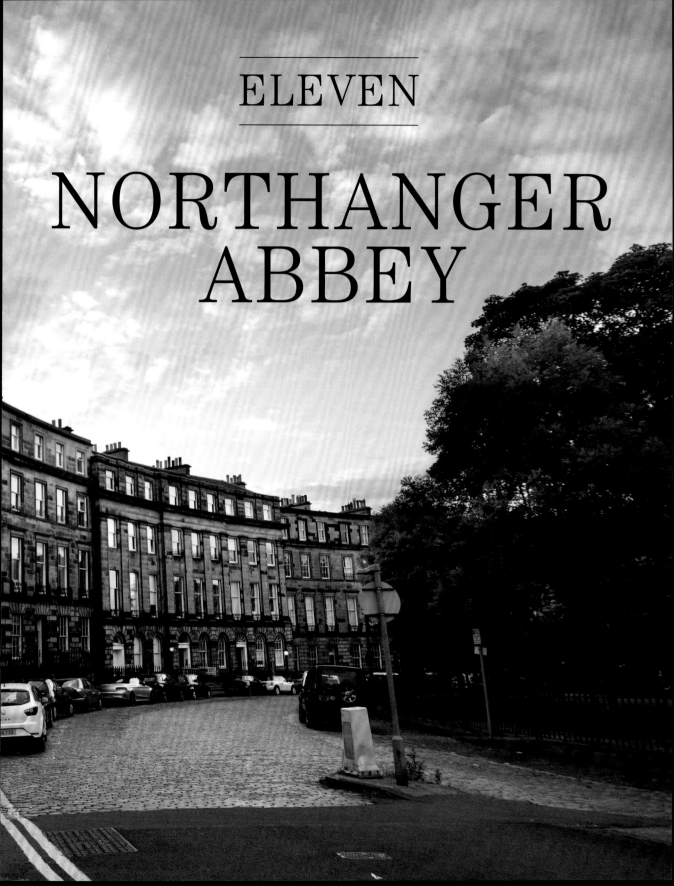

ELEVEN

NORTHANGER ABBEY

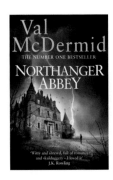

Jane Austen has not a single Scottish character in any of her novels. When I was asked to reimagine *Northanger Abbey* in a contemporary context, I decided to rectify that omission. Not just with the human characters but also with the settings.

The original is set in Bath. I've nothing against Bath – in fact, I have a very lovely honorary doctorate from Bath Spa University – but it's undeniable that nobody goes to Bath for 'the season' these days. I needed to come up with a destination where people spend long enough for the basic mechanics of the plot to get under way, where people go to see and be seen and where romantic promise is in the air. There was only one possibility. Edinburgh in August, when festivals fill every possible performance space, and several highly improbable ones.

Edinburgh was my first city, glamorous and glowering. Arriving by train at Waverley Station – the only one in the world named after a novel – you are confronted by an intimidating soot-black and pale golden skyline of remarkable variety. Its higgledy-piggledy roofline rambles down the hill from the monumental castle, its buildings ranging from the late medieval to the contemporary.

Princes Street Gardens stretches the length of it, only interrupted by William Henry Playfair's neo-classical sandstone art galleries. Walking along Princes Street itself, that skyline acts like a magnet, drawing your eyes upwards. There's no temptation to look in the other direction; most of the shopping side of the street is as depressingly ugly and uniform as every other high street in the country.

Edinburgh was where I fed my teenage appetites. I had a paper delivery round by the time I was twelve, and when I turned fourteen, I got a Sunday job in the local hotel serving breakfast and Sunday lunch. This was my own money, and I spent most of it on books and music.

I'd catch a train to Edinburgh then climb the steep curve of Cockburn Street into the Old Town, dropping in to record shops that sold more than the Top Ten and the *Sound of Music* soundtrack, and boutiques

PREVIOUS SPREAD: Ainslie Place, New Town, Edinburgh, where General Tilney rents a splendid house for the festival.

that reeked of patchouli and offered tie-dye and Indian patterned shirts. Then up North Bridge to James Thin's bookshop opposite the Old College of the university. A formidable lady called Miss Granger ran the children's department and she knew not only her stock but also her clientele. She would remember what she had recommended last and coax out my opinion of it, the better to direct my next purchase. She pointed me towards books that I'd never noticed in the library – Isaac Asimov's *Foundation* trilogy, D.K. Broster's *The Flight of the Heron*. Mary Renault's *The Mask of Apollo*. She encouraged me to expand my reading horizons; I know from what others have told me that she did this for many other readers.

From Thin's, I'd walk along College Street to George IV Bridge. There was a cluster of bookshops around here. A couple sold second-hand paperbacks, and I'd always scour the shelves looking for Agatha Christies I hadn't read yet. Gradually, I began to take a chance on other crime writers, as well as American novelists like Joseph Heller and Carson McCullers.

At that point, my writing ambitions were not directed towards the novel, however. I thought I was going to be a poet or a singer-songwriter. The next Joni Mitchell or Leonard Cohen, ideally. I played guitar and sang in folk clubs and with friends, even daring occasionally to serenade them with one of my own songs. My first properly published piece of writing was a poem published by the *Scotsman* newspaper as one of their three top choices from Scottish school magazines. So the other reason I haunted the George IV Bridge bookshops was that they stocked literary magazines. I dreamed of one day being published in *Lines Review* or *Stand* or *Ambit*. I never managed it, though I did have some poetry published in small magazines when I was at Oxford. But I realised then that I was never going to be a poet; it was too much like hard work to distil an idea or an emotional event into a taut piece of verse.

From the bookshops, I'd walk down into the Grassmarket, still the edgy haunt of drunks and beggars, though the abject and pervasive poverty described by Muriel Spark in *The Prime of Miss Jean Brodie* was gradually giving way to more respectable pubs and the odd fashionable clothes shop such as Campus, where I bought the first winter coat I'd ever paid for with my own money.

As I grew older, sometimes those Saturday afternoons would stretch into the evening. Parties thrown by friends who were studying at the university; plays at the Traverse Theatre written by people who were still alive; and the occasional under-age excursion to a pub where one of my friends was playing an acoustic gig.

I loved Edinburgh; it had been the perfect city for me to navigate my way through my teens. I was determined that my second-hand Austen heroine would find herself there too.

So, seventeen-year-old Cat Morland, improbably innocent of the ways of the world, is whisked away to Edinburgh by her Dorset neighbour, the sophisticated Susie Allen, and her husband, a musical theatre producer. Cat loves the *Twilight* novels and Edinburgh feeds right into her Gothic imagination:

> [Cat] eagerly scanned the neighbourhood, taking in the imposing symmetry of the grey stone buildings that lined the streets, interspersed with orderly tree-lined gardens enclosed by spiked railings. Although the light was barely fading into dusk, in her imagination it was a dark and foggy evening, when this would become a thrillingly ominous landscape. She had come to Edinburgh to be excited, and even at first sight, the city was living up to her expectations.

But Edinburgh during the festival abandons all her gloom and grace, turning instead into a capering crowd of fools. The streets are gaudy with posters advertising comedy and cabaret, plays and poets, singers and strutters of stuff. Masked men robbed of all dignity thrust flyers into the hands of bewildered tourists, while the locals lurk a long way away from the madness. All of which means that Cat and the Allens don't have to wait long for their first encounter with the entertainment.

> The pavement under the triple-arched portico of the Assembly Rooms was busy with people milling around, eyes darting all over the place, eager to spot acquaintances or those they would like to become acquainted with. Posters plastered every surface, over-excited fonts trumpeting the attractions within. Everything clamoured for Cat's attention and she clung nervously to Susie's arm as they pushed through the crowds to get inside.

St Bernard's Crescent with its private gardens.

The scrum of people seemed to grow thicker the further they penetrated the building. Mr Allen had spoken of the grace and elegance of the interior, explaining how it had been restored to its eighteenth-century glory. 'They've kept the perfect proportions and returned it to its original style of decoration, right down to the chandeliers and the gold leaf on the ceiling roses,' he'd told them over their early dinner. Cat had been eager to see it for herself, but it was too crowded to form any sense of how it looked. In between the heads and the hoardings she could catch odd glimpses here and there, but it formed a bewildering kaleidoscope of images. The sole impression she had was of hundreds of people determined to see and be seen on their way to and from an assortment of performances.

'I know where we're going.' Susie had to raise her voice to be heard in the throng. She half-led, half-dragged Cat through the crowd until they finally reached their destination. Susie handed over their tickets and they were admitted to the auditorium.

This was not Cat's initiation into live performance. She'd regularly attended performances in the village hall and even, occasionally, at the Arts Centre in Dorchester. She knew what to expect. Rows of seats, a soft mumble of conversation, a curtained proscenium arch.

Instead, she was thrust into a hot humid mass of bodies that filled the space around a small raised dais at one end of the packed room. Through the gloom, she could see some chairs, but they were all taken. What remained was standing room only. Standing room so tightly packed that Cat was convinced if she passed out, nobody would know until they all began to file out and she crumpled to the floor.

I'm not making this up, you know. Well, not the ambience, just the story … Cat's cultural journey leads her to romance, when she encounters handsome Henry Tilney at a Scottish country dancing class, and she searches for him in vain at the tented village of the Book Festival in Charlotte Square Gardens and at an al fresco performance of *Cupcakes to Die For* in the Botanic Gardens before running into him again at a grand Highland Ball in a Georgian mansion in the New Town. Cat became my surrogate in some of the places I love in the city and its environs.

The other advantage of choosing Edinburgh was that it allowed me a way round the problem of communication. Often in Austen, key plot elements have space to happen because it takes time for news to travel. Or miscommunication leads to misunderstanding. In our digital world, though, it often feels like there's no hiding place. Except that there are still significant areas of the Scottish Borders where there is no phone signal. Add to that a paranoid householder who refuses to turn on the Wi-Fi router except when he is using it himself, and Cat is rendered virtually incommunicado by moving Northanger Abbey to the Borders to sit alongside the other medieval abbeys such as Melrose, Jedburgh and Kelso. For Cat, obsessed with the idea of vampires and ghosts, it's a sort of creepy paradise.

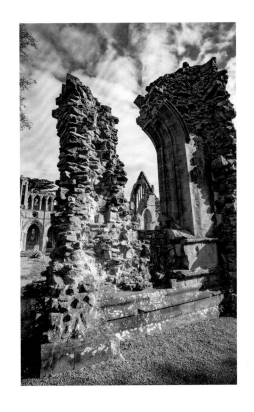

> Cat turned a large black iron ring set in the studded door and it swung open silently. They stepped into an ancient hall with a vast stone fireplace, dominated by the wide sweep of a stone staircase that split halfway up and led to either side of a gallery that surrounded the hall. Faded rugs were scattered on the stone flags and the walls were hung with gloomy landscapes dominated by dark crags and ominously tumbling water. Her heart soared. This was what she had dreamed of, this was what she had craved. This was no genteel converted church, it was a fortified house, a castle almost, steeped in history.

Of course, none of Cat's Gothic fantasies of sinister hauntings and a blood-stained history are reflected in reality. But I did have some fun along the way, and judging by the reaction of even the most ardent Jane Austen fan, so did the readers who came along for the ride.

A bizarre footnote:

When I'm writing, I like to be able to conjure up a mental picture of the place I'm writing about. When I sent Cat and the Allens to Edinburgh, I was still living in Northumberland so I did some online research on the

ABOVE: The ruins of Dryburgh Abbey (detail).

PREVIOUS SPREAD: Charlotte Square, Edinburgh; the Edinburgh International Book Festival by day and night.

websites of Edinburgh estate agents. I found the perfect flat overlooking the tree-lined oasis of Queen Street Gardens; even though it was on the market at a ridiculous price.

> Mr Allen liked to live well, and he always took comfortable lodgings for his August pilgrimage. This year, he'd rented a three-bedroomed flat towards the West End of Queen Street which came with that contemporary Edinburgh equivalent of the Holy Grail – a parking permit. By the time they'd found a parking space that matched it then lugged their bags up several flights of stairs, none of them had appetite or energy for anything more than a good night's sleep.

A year after I finished the book, I wanted to move back to Scotland, to live in Edinburgh. When I started looking for somewhere to live, the flat I'd come to think of as the Allens' place was still on the market, though now it carried a much-reduced price tag.

> Reader, I bought the flat …

The ruins of Dryburgh Abbey in the Borders (LEFT) and a typical Borders fortified country house – just the sort of place I imagined for my Northanger Abbey!

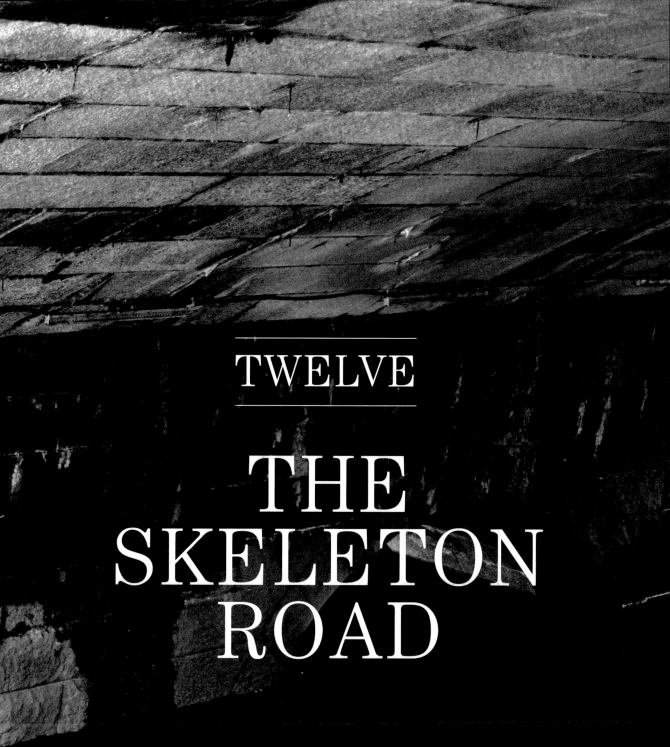

TWELVE

THE
SKELETON
ROAD

When I was growing up, we lived on the same street as the former Kirkcaldy High School building. It was an imposing square sandstone building dating back to 1843. But by the time we moved there, it had become part of Kirkcaldy Technical College, and a new modern extension complete with a tower block was being built. I used to walk past the old building and envy the college students those spacious classrooms with their high ceilings and tall windows.

The school I joined when I was eleven was a functional modern block built in the shape of the letter H. It was less than ten years old but already it was showing signs of wear and tear. The cloakrooms were horrible – dark and ugly, always smelly and overcrowded. The classrooms were cramped, with poor acoustics. Only the science labs felt spacious.

The library was a decent size and well-stocked, with a private study area for fifth- and sixth-year pupils. But the school had a very narrow idea of what private study meant. I was once bawled out by the school head for reading a novel in private study; it was on the English syllabus, but that didn't seem to matter. 'Nuvvels' were too much like fun.

But we had a proud academic record, regularly winning more bursaries to Edinburgh University than any other state school in Scotland. But it wasn't a hothouse of learning. Extra-curricular activities were regarded as a key part of school. Sport, music, drama, debating, science, chess and bridge all had their after-school societies.

I played hockey. I was in the first XI and I also played for the East District team. I even had a Scottish Schoolgirls trial. We had one season where, according to our gym teacher, we were the only undefeated school team in Scotland. I took that very personally, because I was the goalkeeper.

There was one aspect of our sporting lives that probably never crossed the minds of our teachers. The schools we played against were not all state schools. We regularly faced opposition from private schools in Edinburgh and elsewhere. We were confronted with facilities that

outstripped ours in almost every respect (though we still beat them on the pitch!). More than that, though – we caught sight of beautiful, elegant buildings that seemed to me to belong in works of fiction rather than reality.

I imagined what they were like on the inside. High ceilings. Wide staircases. Wood floors that echoed to the clattering of school shoes. The smell of chalk dust. Toilets with mahogany stalls and high cisterns with dangling chains. And basements with boiler rooms and mysterious hidden places. Buildings designed for mystery and adventure.

Of course, they were probably nothing like that. Inside, they likely had more common ground with Kirkcaldy High School than difference. But the fantasy remained intact, buried somewhere in the back of my mind.

Years later, a serendipitous book review led me to *The Night Climbers of Cambridge*, a facsimile edition of a book first published in 1937 under the pseudonym of Whipplesnaith. It outlined, complete with photographs, the bizarre hobby of nocturnal free climbing on the buildings of Cambridge colleges. Something sparked my imagination. That's generally how books start with me. An anecdote, a throwaway line,

ABOVE: Kirkcaldy Police HQ (opposite the former High School) where Karen started out as a police cadet.

PREVIOUS SPREAD: Jamaica Bridge, Glasgow. A suitably atmospheric place for a sinister encounter.

something that intrigues me with its oddness.

I wondered where it might lead if a modern urban explorer were to stumble upon a skeleton in an apparently inaccessible area of a roof. Obviously it would involve a cold case investigation, and I already had a cold case detective in the shape of Karen Pirie. But the story couldn't be set in Cambridge, for her jurisdiction is Scotland. I started thinking about Edinburgh and recalled those marvellous school buildings with their turrets and pinnacles. There were several candidates that suggested themselves to me but the one I kept coming back to was Donaldson's School for the Deaf. It sits on the main A8 just outside the city centre; we often passed it on the hockey bus.

It's a Victorian Gothic take on Tudor manor houses, designed by William Henry Playfair, one of the most distinguished Scottish architects of the nineteenth century. When Queen Victoria opened it in 1850, she's said to have remarked that it was more impressive than her own palaces. It's built round a quadrangle with imposing towers on each corner. The towers themselves are surmounted by four smaller towers. It had been standing empty for a decade before developers began to turn it into luxury apartments for millionaires.

The perfect model for my imaginary body dump.

Fraser had driven past the John Drummond countless times, marvelling at the fact that from a distance it still looked as impressive as ever, even after standing empty for the best part of twenty years. It was an

The imposing façade of Donaldson's School for the Deaf and those tempting turrets.

Edinburgh landmark, its elaborate façade impressively dominating what amounted to a small park beside one of the southbound arterial roads. For years, the sheer scale of any redevelopment of the abandoned private school had daunted developers. But the exponential expansion of the city's student population had created more pressure on accommodation and more profits for developers with the nerve to go for major projects.

And so Fraser was stuck on this decaying roof on a cold Saturday morning. He began making his tentative way round the perimeter, dividing his attention between the parapet and the roof, dictating occasional notes into the voice-activated recorder clipped to his hi-vis tabard. When he came to the first of the tall mock-Gothic pinnacles that stood at each corner of the roof, he paused, assessing it carefully. It was about four metres tall, not much more than a metre in diameter at its base, rising in a steep cone to its apex. The exterior was decorated with extravagant stone carvings. Why would you do that, Fraser wondered. Even the Victorians must have had better ways to spend their money. So why would you choose that? All that over-the-top detail where nobody was ever going to see it up close, balls and curlicues stark against the sky. Some had fallen off over the years. Luckily nobody had been standing underneath when that had happened. At roof level, there was a small arch in the stonework, presumably to provide access to the interior of the pinnacle. Access for the youngest and smallest of the mason's apprentices, Fraser reckoned. He doubted he could even get his shoulders through the widest span of the arch. Still, he really should take a look.

He lay down in the gutter, switched on the head torch on his hard hat and edged forward. Once his head was inside, he was able to make a surprisingly good assessment of the interior. The floor was covered with herringbone brick; the interior walls were brick, sagging slightly in places where the mortar had crumbled away, but held in place by the weight pressing down from above. A bundle of feathers in one corner marked where a pigeon had lost the battle with its own stupidity. The air was tainted with an acrid whiff that Fraser attributed to whatever vermin had visited the building. Rats, bats, mice. Whatever.

Satisfied that there was nothing else of note, Fraser backed out and eased himself back to his feet. He tugged his tabard straight and continued his inspection. Second side. Second turret. Don't look down. Third side. A section of crenellated parapet so decayed it appeared to be held together by faith alone.

The third pinnacle loomed like a place of safety. On his hands and knees, Fraser switched on the head torch again and thrust his head inside the access arch. This time, what he saw made him rear up so abruptly that he smacked his head on the back of the arch, sending his hard hat tumbling across the floor, the beam of light careering around madly before it finally rocked itself still.

Fraser whimpered. At last he'd found something on a roof that was scarier than the height. Grinning at him across the brickwork was a skull, lying on a scatter of bones that had clearly once been a human being.

A stark contrast to this location comes in the literal shape of Gartcosh Campus. The building itself is based on the very building blocks of existence – DNA barcodes. Light and shade, angles and materials were chosen to reflect the coding that's familiar to anyone who has even a passing familiarity with the forensic use of DNA. The campus brings together the Scottish Crime and Drug Enforcement Agency, Serious Organised Crime Agency, Her Majesty's Revenue and Customs, Scottish Police Services Authority Forensic Services, Crown Office Procurator Fiscal Service and UK Border Agency into a single site where it can support the work of Police Scotland. There are offices, labs, meeting rooms and breakout areas. All you need for a modern investigative hub.
And yet …

So early on a Sunday morning, there wasn't much traffic and she made record time to the brand new Scottish Police Authority's Serious Crime Campus. It sat in what Karen liked to think of as Scotland's answer to the Bermuda triangle – the godforsaken area that lay between the M80, the M73 and the M8. It had been christened the Gartcosh Business Interchange to make it sound exciting and dynamic. It would, she thought, take more than rebranding to wipe

the local population's memory of the massive strip mill and steel works that had employed getting on for a thousand local men whose working lives had effectively ended when British Steel closed the plant in 1986. A generation later, the scars remained.

The new building was a dramatic addition to the view. Its white concrete and tinted glass exterior looked like giant barcodes embedded in the landscape at odd angles to each other. The first time she'd seen it, Karen had been baffled by it, tempted to dismiss it as a piece of self-indulgence on the part of the architects. But Phil, who'd been reading about it online, had explained that it was in the shape of a human chromosome and that the barcode effect was meant to represent DNA. 'It's a metaphor,' he'd said. Grudgingly, she'd accepted that since part of the building would be housing the forensic science arm of Police Scotland, there was a point to the design. She was just glad that nobody was suggesting she should work inside a bloody metaphor.

One good thing about Sunday was the parking. The government wanted everyone to be green and use public transport to commute to work. So when new buildings went up, it was policy to create far fewer parking spaces than there were employees. According to one of Karen's former colleagues, Gartcosh had two hundred and fifty spaces for twelve hundred employees. But those employees had mostly been relocated to Gartcosh from somewhere else in the Central Belt. And very few of those somewhere elses had public transport links to Gartcosh. 'Some folk get to their work before seven o'clock, just to get a parking space,' he'd told her. Others swore a lot and churned up the grass verges of the surrounding roads. It wasn't going to change government policy but it did make them feel better.

Inside the building, everything was still shiny and new except for the people. They were as dishevelled, nerdy and grumpy as ever.

You really can't please all of the people all of the time …

The Police Scotland Gartcosh Campus from the air, modelled on a strand of DNA. Home of the forensic labs, among other units.

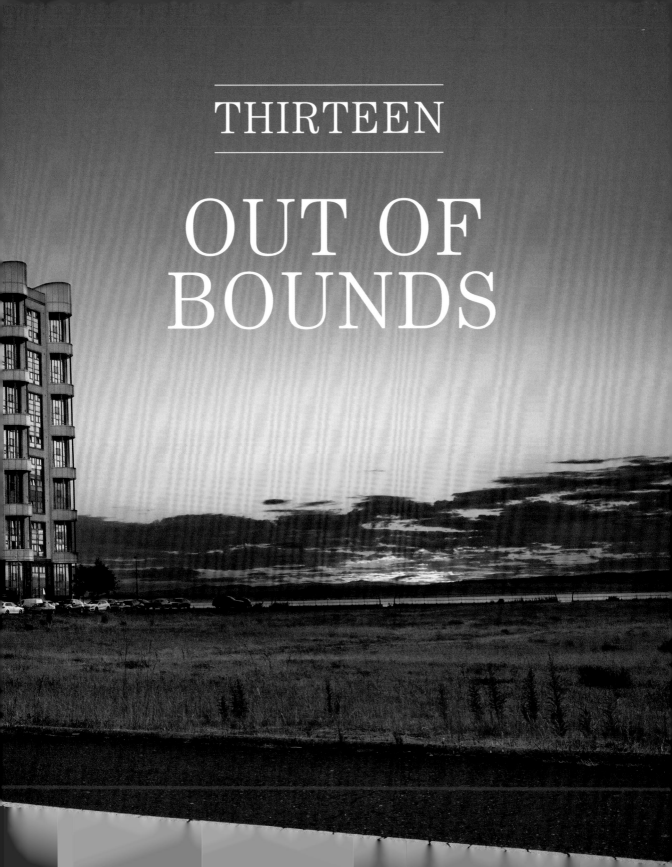

THIRTEEN

OUT OF BOUNDS

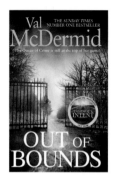

When I moved back to Scotland in 2014 I was already thinking about the next Karen Pirie novel, even though *The Skeleton Road* had only just been published. That's how series work for me. I never write two books back to back with the same characters – I get bored too easily – but invariably, by the time I'm coming towards the end of a novel featuring regular characters, ideas for their next case start bubbling up.

Out of Bounds marked significant changes for Karen. The creation of Police Scotland, an amalgamation of the eight regional forces, meant she was no longer based in Fife. I promoted her to Detective Chief Inspector and gave her a nationwide remit as head of the fictitious Historic Cases Unit. A unit that consists solely of Karen and the dim but good-hearted Detective Constable Jason Murray.

I decided to base them in the Gayfield Square police station in the centre of Edinburgh, mostly because I like Karen and Jason far too much to condemn them to the wilderness of Gartcosh, however modern and high-tech it might be. I let her walk up the hill to enjoy the remarkable view from the steps on General Register House of Edinburgh landmarks rather than the distant prospect of motorway junctions. Sometimes it just feels good to give my characters some pleasure to sit alongside the pain I put them through.

The other change Karen has to cope with is a personal one. She's struggling with the grief of a close bereavement and the way she's chosen to deal with it is to move from the familiarity of her home town to the less well-known terrain of Edinburgh. She's deliberately chosen a modern flat with a constantly changing view of the Forth estuary including a distant prospect of the imposing trio of bridges that link Fife and the Lothians. It's a place with no memories.

But that's not nearly enough to bring her peace. The other casualty of her loss is sleep.

She walked. Whenever sleep slipped from her grasp, she walked. It occurred to her that her life had come to resemble the first draft of an advertising script for Guinness or Stella Artois. 'She walks. That's what she does.' Except that there was no brightly lit pub full of cheery faces waiting to greet her at the end of her wanderings.

Sometimes, if she was tired enough, sleep would creep up on her and pin her to the bed like a wrestler faster and stronger than she was. But it never lasted long. As soon as exhaustion relaxed its hold on her, she'd surface again, eyes gritty and swollen, mouth dry and tasting of death.

And so she would walk. Along the breakwater, tall apartment blocks to her left, the choppy waters of the Firth of Forth on her right, the night breeze filling her nostrils with salt and seaweed. Then she'd turn inland, past the twenty-four-hour Asda and across the main drag into the old village of Newhaven. She'd pick random routes through the huddled streets of fishermen's cottages, then work her way inland and upwards, always trying to choose streets and alleys and quiet back lanes that she'd never entered before.

That was part of the point. She had chosen to move to Edinburgh precisely because it was unfamiliar. She'd grown up a mere forty-minute train journey away, but the capital had always been exotic.

ABOVE: Gayfield Square Police Station where Karen Pirie works.

PREVIOUS SPREAD: Western Breakwater flats, Leith, on the Firth of Forth. Karen has a flat here with fabulous views.

The big city. The place for a special day out. She'd only been familiar with the main streets of the centre until work had started to bring her here from time to time, opening up small windows on disconnected corners. But still, Edinburgh was not a place laden with memories to ambush her in the way that her home town was. Deciding to live here had felt like a project. Learning the city one street at a time might take her mind off the grief and the pain.

And as Karen familiarised herself with the city, so too did I. I extended my range outwards from the city centre, learning unfamiliar districts, picking my way through the half-hidden lanes and by-ways that worm their way through the streets and squares of both Old and New Town, making discoveries on every walk. Like Karen, I came across surprises, but none quite like the one she found in the early hours of one chilly night.

She was plotting a zigzag course along the edge of Leith when she came across the start of the Restalrig Railway Path. She'd encountered the far end of it once before, when she'd found herself down by the shore in Portobello. The disused railway line had been tarmacked over and turned into an off-road route for cyclists and walkers to cut across the city. Street lamps stretched into the distance, giving a sense of safety to what would otherwise have been a dark and uninviting cutting slicing through some of the poorer areas of the city.

She thought about the hidden ways that snaked through the city. Edinburgh had more than its fair share, from those streets in the old town that had simply been buried beneath new rows of houses, to the closes and stairways and ginnels that made a honeycomb of the old town. Here, there was no clue to what the path had once been except steep banks of untended undergrowth and the occasional straggly tree trying to make something of itself in unpromising circumstances. Every now and then, a heavy iron bridge crossed the path, carrying a road above her head. The stone walls supporting the bridges were covered in graffiti tags, their bright colours muted in the low-level lighting. Not exactly art, Karen thought, but better than nothing.

She rounded a curve and was surprised by the glow of some kind of fire underneath the next bridge. She slowed, taking in what lay

Restalrig Railway Path.

ahead of her. A knot of men huddled round low tongues of flame. Overcoats and beanie hats, heavy jackets and caps with earflaps, shoulders hunched against the night. As she drew nearer, she realised the centre of their attention was what looked like a garden incinerator fuelled by scrap wood. And what she'd taken for beanies were actually kufi prayer hats.

It didn't occur to her to be nervous of half a dozen men of Middle Eastern appearance gathered round a makeshift fire in the middle of the night. Not in the way she would have been if it had been a bunch of drunks or teens off their heads on glue or drugs. She wasn't heedless of risk, but she had a good estimation of the air of confidence and competence she exuded. Besides, she reckoned she was pretty good at telling the difference between 'unusual' and 'threatening'. She still held fast to that conviction, in spite of the unlikely event that had robbed her life of its meaning.

As she approached, one of the men spotted her and nudged his neighbour. The word went round the group and the low mutter of conversation ceased. By the time she'd broached the loose circle around the flames, they'd fallen silent, a ring of expressionless faces and blank brown eyes fixed on her. She held her hands out to warm them – who could begrudge her that in the chill of night? – and gave them a nod of acknowledgement. They stood around in an awkward grouping, nonplussed men and a woman who could afford to be relaxed because she believed she had nothing left to lose.

A typical Old Town vennel, the sort of place Karen discovers on her night wanderings.

The men are a group of Syrian refugees, strangers in a strange land. And because Karen feels kinship with them, a bond is forged that runs through the book like a thread.

But Karen's writ runs well beyond the capital and this book takes her to places with very different ambiences. I placed a corpse on a bench on the twelve-mile nature trail that encircles Loch Leven, with a view of Castle Island where Mary Queen of Scots was held prisoner for the best part of a year and abdicated in favour of her infant son.

In nearby Kinross, I took one of those liberties that fiction makes possible. I transplanted one of my favourite Edinburgh pubs, the Bailie, from the corner of St Stephen Street in Edinburgh to a road where no pub sits. But the Bailie would fit there very nicely, it seemed to me, and that would be a civilised place for my victim to enjoy his last drink.

I let Karen enjoy one of the best fish suppers in Fife – which is no small boast, since Fife boasts the official best fish and chip shop in Scotland – at the Ship Inn in Limekilns. I have her send Jason down Leith Walk to pick up lunchtime curries from the social enterprise café Punjabi Junction. And I had a man who wishes her harm stand along the bar from her and Jason in Ryrie's pub outside Haymarket Station. All landmarks that locals know and visitors can enjoy.

But not everywhere in Scotland is lovely. And Karen sometimes gets the chance to express disappointment and distaste that she may or may not share with me …

ABOVE: Fish and chips at the Ship Inn in Limekilns.

RIGHT: Loch Leven, and the author assuming the role of the victim on its shores.

Linlithgow town centre always struck Karen as a random act of violence by town planners. It was hard not to be charmed by the striking romantic ruin of the late medieval palace, or the clutch of interesting and attractive buildings from the eighteenth and nineteenth centuries lining one side of the main street. Then, slapped down right in the heart of that street was one of the ugliest brutalist blocks of flats she'd ever seen. It overlooked the market place, with its statue of St Michael, promising to be *kinde to straingers*. Somebody had been very unkind indeed to the citizens of Linlithgow.

Karen even gets to cross the country to Glasgow to interview witnesses. And that's allowed me to revisit Byres Road in the West End, a location I first used way back in those early Lindsay Gordon novels. Here it is more recently:

Liz Dunleavy always felt a sense of homecoming when she walked through the door of the original Hair Apparent. It hadn't always been like that. At first, she'd felt like a bit of a chancer. The inhabitants of the red sandstone tenement streets of the West End of Glasgow who weren't still students were mostly academics or media professionals. Liz often said to her clients that you could open a bookshop stocked only with the publications of the people who lived in the G12 postcode. By contrast, Liz had grown up in the East End of the city, in a tenement that had dodged slum clearance by the skin of its rotten teeth. Neither parent had any expectations of their six children except that they would likely be more trouble than they were worth. What Liz had lacked in advantages, she'd more than made up for in ambition, and her own transformation had been her greatest work of the stylist's art.

ABOVE: Punjabi Junction on Leith Walk, Edinburgh.

RIGHT: Linlithgow town centre. Old and new.

When she'd opened up her first salon, the location had been at the unfashionable end of Byres Road, but the world had changed to her advantage. Now Hair Apparent was surrounded by the kind of cafés where you could get any beverage except a straightforward cup of coffee; an artisan bakery; a handful of reasonable places to eat; estate agents staffed by tense and rapacious young people; and pubs that been stripped to the bone and reconstructed in the image that attracted students and young professionals trying to stay in contact with their misspent youth.

Yes, even Scotland has succumbed to the coffee revolution. But more of that later ...

EDINBURGH IS AS RUTH

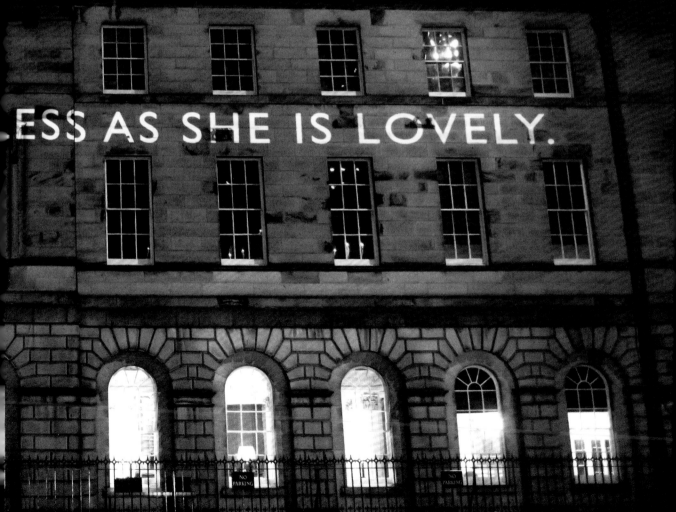

FOURTEEN

MESSAGE FROM THE SKIES

The brief was straightforward. 'We'd like you to write a short story, between 2500 and 3000 words long. It has to be capable of being broken up into twelve sections. It should reflect Edinburgh's status as the first UNESCO City of Literature. We'd like it to have suspense and maybe even a murder or two, since it's you.'

I can probably do that, I thought. 'And how is this to be published?'

'We're going to project it on landmarks and buildings around the city centre. It'll be a sort of guided walk. It'll run from New Year's Day till Burns Night. Oh, and nothing like this has ever been attempted anywhere.'

Straightforward. Aye, right.

But in the end, somehow 2018 in Edinburgh was hanselled in with my words projected on a dozen sites around the city centre. This was the first *Message from the Skies*, a joint project between Edinburgh's Hogmanay and the Edinburgh International Book Festival, aimed at bringing together writers and artists in other media to create an annual New Year spectacular. I called my inaugural episode 'New Year Resurrection'. It took months of planning, a wide range of expertise and intense collaboration. The collaboration bit was one of the major challenges for me. Writers spend most of their time in a room by themselves. We do not generally play well with others.

Having agreed to the challenge, the first thing I had to figure out was a story. The title of the project is a quote from a Robert Burns poem, 'Sketch: New Year's Day. To Mrs Dunlop'. It reads:

The voice of Nature loudly cries,

And many a message from the skies,

That something in us never dies:

That was the first pricking of an idea. Perhaps I should be looking to the past for my inspiration. Writers, after all, never die while their work is still enjoyed. But when I started looking at the writers' Edinburgh honours,

I was struck by a phenomenon. They were, almost without exception, men.

I thought back over my years of reading. There was no shortage of exceptional Scottish women writers, going back to Joanna Baillie, a successful poet and playwright in the mid-eighteenth century, whose work was regularly and successfully produced on the London stage. And I remembered Susan Edmonstone Ferrier, a novelist writing at about the same time as Jane Austen. I'd read her debut, *Marriage*, when I was an undergraduate studying the development of the novel. It wasn't on the syllabus, but I'd come across a reference to it in some critical essay or other and, thanks to the all-encompassing collection of the Bodleian Library, I was able to get my hands on it. I vaguely remembered it having a lot in common with Austen – the social satire and the sharp observation. But I also recalled Ferrier having a broader canvas. For example, her servants had personalities and had a role to play within the story.

While Austen had grown in stature and reputation, Susan Ferrier had disappeared without trace. I revisited *Marriage* to check my recollection of its pleasures and grew more puzzled. Frankly, *Marriage* is at least as

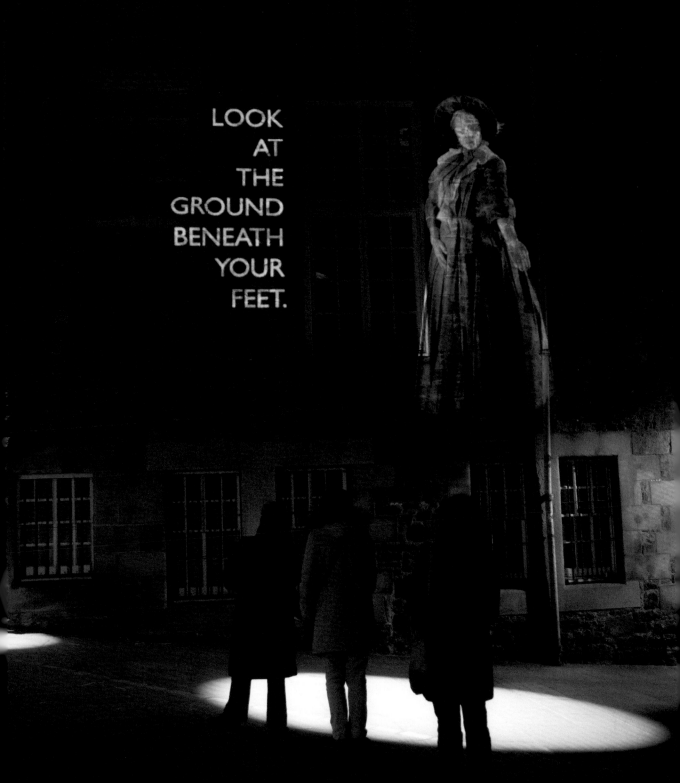

good as many other Victorian novels that are still well-known and well-read. I decided it was time to redress the balance and try to restore Susan's reputation.

And along the way, I'd strike a blow for the recognition of other Scottish women writers.

I had a fabulous backdrop for my story. The only problem was how to narrow down the potential sites. Edinburgh teems with grand buildings and vistas, after all. But the dramaturg I was working with, Philip Howard, hit on the solution to that dilemma. I should make the story site-specific. As far as possible, the places I chose should have some relevance to the story I was telling. At first, I wasn't sure how this would work. But a little research offered us some amazingly serendipitous discoveries.

Susan herself was born in Lady Stair's Close, home of the Scottish Writers' Museum (celebrating the works of Robert Louis Stevenson, Walter Scott and Robert Burns …). The paving slabs of the close feature quotes from Scottish writers. The men outnumber the women about eight to one. I could feel my narrative taking shape.

Susan died in her brother's house in Albany Street, in the New Town; a perfect stopping-off point between the Conan Doyle pub and Robert Louis Stevenson's house. And she's buried in St Cuthbert's Churchyard in the shadow of the castle. Even better for our purposes, the Ferrier family grave looks like a pair of Gothic doorways.

And the final link in the chain was that 2018 was the bicentenary of the publication of *Marriage*. It was also the centenary of the birth of Muriel Spark – in my opinion, probably the greatest Scottish novelist of the twentieth century. Enter stage left, Muriel, to take up the final part of the narrative in the Grassmarket, where the iconic Miss Jean Brodie takes her girls to show them the foreign country that is poverty.

The story opens right at the Heart of Midlothian, in Parliament Square outside St Giles' Cathedral. The text was projected on to the Signet Library, the very core of the Scottish legal establishment.

When I was six years old, my daddy took me to see a man being hanged, right where you're standing now. Half the city was here. Forty thousand people turned up to see Deacon Brodie swing from a gallows tree he'd designed himself. A proper eighteenth-century gentleman, or so everybody thought.

Lady Stair's Close and the Writers' Museum with the ghost of Susan Ferrier.

But somehow, in a small city where houses crowded close and people knew every noisy detail of their neighbours' lives, Brodie managed to keep his secrets. Not a single member of the Edinburgh establishment was aware that he had not one, but two mistresses who between them had given birth to five of his children.

It takes a lot of money to keep a secret as big as that. Brodie's answer was simple. He was the city locksmith. So he made extra copies of the keys that unlocked the doors of the rich and comfortable. And in the night, he crept into their homes and their offices and robbed the very citizens he rubbed shoulders with in business and politics. When they discovered how he'd bamboozled them, there was only ever going to be one outcome.

I saw Deacon Brodie's last dance from my daddy's shoulders. Maybe you think that's a terrible thing to show a child. But that's Edinburgh for you. Don't be fooled by the superficial charms. Edinburgh is as ruthless as she is lovely. Here, now, at the turning of the year, when Janus-faced January looks to the past as well as the future, we're held fast in the frosty embrace of Edinburgh. Anything can happen in these pends and yards, these courts and lands, these vennels and closes, these wynds and braes, these markets in hay and grass and lawn. And flesh.

This is a city of opposites. Good and evil. Old and new. High life and low life. Respectable … and very definitely unrespectable. But most of all, it's a city of stories.

The Bank of Scotland building, and the screen revealing the Scott monument on Princes Street.

SO THE ONE WHO GOT THE
GREAT GOTHIC PINNACLE
TOWERING OVER PRINCES STREET
WAS WALTER SCOTT, PAID FOR BY
A KIND OF NINETEENTH CENTURY
KICKSTARTER.

EXCEPT THAT THE CITY COUNCIL
COMPLETELY MISJUDGED HOW
MUCH PEOPLE WANTED IT AND
THEY ENDED UP HAVING
LITERALLY TO GO DOOR TO DOOR
BEGGING FOR FUNDS. IF YOU
GAVE A GUINEA OR MORE, YOU
GOT A PRINT OF THE MONUMENT,
JUST LIKE ANY OTHER
CROWDFUNDER.

IF IT HAD BEEN UP TO HIM,
I'M SURE I'D HAVE BEEN UP THERE
BESIDE HIM.

That wasn't
as satisfying as I thought it would be.
Maybe that's because Walter himself
was a great supporter of women writers.

These days, he'd be
one of those writers whose blurbs
are all over other people's
book jackets.

The story continued on the façade of the National Library of Scotland, then moved to Lady Stair's Close, where viewers discovered who their narrator was.

> I was born right here where you're standing, in Lady Stair's Close. My name is Susan Edmonstone Ferrier. You're none the wiser, are you? I am – I was, I suppose I must say, since I've been dead since 1854 – a writer. My first novel, *Marriage*, was a vivid and wryly satirical account of Scottish social life containing acerbic views about marriage and women's education. It was published seven years after Jane Austen's debut. According to my Wikipedia page, my books form a trilogy – 'an extended inquiry on the subjects of nation, history, and the evolution of female consciousness'.
>
> As if the thousands of readers who read my books gave a damn about that. What matters is that they loved the stories I wrote. They adored my characters and their adventures. I know this because they told me so. If Twitter had been invented, I'd have had a blue tick and a damn sight more followers than Walter Scott.
>
> But instead, like so many of my sisters, I disappeared …
>
> Who killed us off? Who rubbed us out of the picture? Who decided the Walters and the Roberts and the Jameses and all the rest of them should get all the limelight?
>
> THE CRITICS
>
> Well, tonight I'm back from the other side to set things right. I'm here to put the women back where they belong. Front and centre. Tonight it's time for resurrection. For resurrection and REVENGE.

And so Susan sets off on a mission to kill the critics. From outside the Bank of Scotland, she demolishes the Scott Monument and replaces it with her own statue. A series of graffiti panels all the way up the Scotsman Steps – a flight I'd often clattered down towards the station to catch the last train home – continue her diatribe and culminate in a series of dramatic silhouettes of bloody murder under the Waterloo Place viaduct.

The most controversial scene took place at the Conan Doyle pub on Picardy Place, right by the Sherlock creator's birthplace.

FORGET GREYFRIARS BOBBY. IT'S A RIDICULOUS STORY AND IT'S NOT EVEN TRUE.

Every good killer needs a good detective. And Edinburgh is where the inspiration for Sherlock Holmes struck Arthur Conan Doyle. Who was born across the street and baptized right here in the Edinburgh Catholic cathedral. His professor at Edinburgh University liked to show off his deductive skills, and Conan Doyle leapt on the idea as a gimmick for his detective. Crowds queued up outside the offices of his publisher to get the next instalment in the adventures of Sherlock Holmes. Hysterical fans wept when they thought there would be no more stories. Does that remind you of anyone?

That's right. J.K. Rowling. Harry Potter fans standing in line outside bookshops, waiting for midnight to strike, so they could get their hands on his next adventure.

And J.K.'s created her own detective now. Cormoran Strike, every bit as distinctive as the man in the deerstalker, and already followed by his own army of fans.

Time to strike another blow for us women, I think.

And then as if by magic, the pub name changed from 'The Conan Doyle' to 'The J.K. Rowling'. But we didn't just change the name of the pub via the projection; we persuaded the pub landlords to change the name and the painted pub sign on the other side of the building for the duration of *Message from the Skies*. The outraged outcry was loud; our pleasure, considerable.

The story continued, eventually ending up in the churchyard of Greyfriars Kirk, where Muriel Spark delivers the final speech:

> Forget Greyfriars Bobby. It's a ridiculous story and it's not even true. What is much more important is that this is where the National Covenant was signed three hundred and eighty years ago. It was a sort of declaration of independence; an oath to do whatever it took to stop the Catholic Church holding any sway over the Scots. A nonsense, really. If you're going to do a thing, you should do it thoroughly. If you're going to be a Christian, you may as well be a Catholic. But the covenant led to bloody civil war and when the

The spell has been cast!

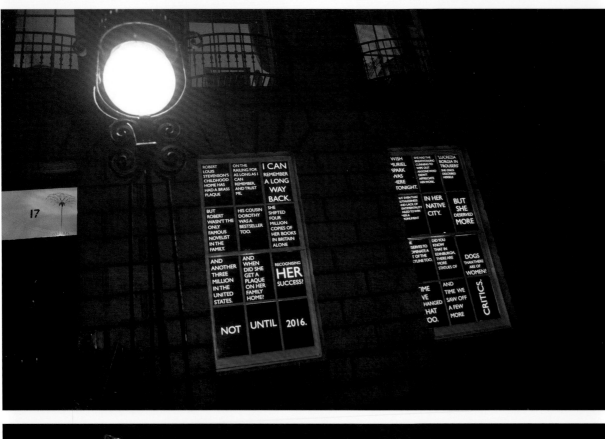

Covenanters lost their military fight, more than a thousand of them were held prisoner in this very kirkyard. A practical demonstration of what I explained to Susan. If you're going to engage in violence, you have to be very sure you're going to win.

And so this year of our Lord 2018 will be the year of Muriel Spark. A hundred years after my birth, you won't be able to miss me. I have never been a woman to whom things happen. I do all the happenings. Now, pay attention at the back!

[*On the walls of the kirkyard, one after another, the names light up in neon*]

Welcome to Edinburgh, UNESCO City of Literature. Home to Muriel Spark, Robert Louis Stevenson, Susan Ferrier, Walter Scott, J.K. Rowling, Robert Burns, Joanna Baillie, James Hogg, Kate Atkinson, Arthur Conan Doyle, Naomi Mitchison, Irvine Welsh, Dorothy Dunnett, Kenneth Grahame, Louise Welsh, Ian Rankin, Val McDermid, Alexander McCall Smith.

All through the cold dark nights of January, the *Message from the Skies* lit up the Edinburgh Streets. Many thousands of people followed the trail – some more than once! – and as far as I could discover, they enjoyed themselves. Me? I was delighted to have been given the chance to tell a different kind of story in a different way.

W.H. Auden remarked that poetry changes nothing. But sometimes plastering buildings with bits of prose can have a tangible effect. When the Virago publishing house heard about the 'New Year's Resurrection' of Susan Ferrier, they decided to publish a new edition of *Marriage*. Thanks to our midwinter endeavour, a new generation of readers have access to an almost-forgotten novel.

The story draws towards its close on the windows of Robert Louis Stevenson's childhood home and in St Cuthbert's churchyard.

FIFTEEN

BROKEN GROUND

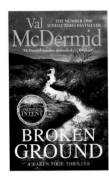

The fifth novel to feature cold case cop Karen Pirie opens in 1944 with two men burying a couple of wooden crates in a peat bog in Wester Ross. When the crates are unearthed seventy-four years later, what's inside sparks a new investigation for Karen and her colleagues.

The idea for this book started, as is so often the case, with a throwaway line. I was reading a biography of Josephine Tey, the Scottish writer who spent most of her life in Inverness, when I read a brief sentence referring to the fact that during the war, the Highlands were a restricted zone. I'd known that, but as with so many things, I'd forgotten I knew it. To enter the area north of the Great Glen required a special pass. And even if you lived there, your movements were strictly limited without the right paperwork.

I thought there might be the makings of a story there. I knew Wester Ross reasonably well – I'd holidayed there, most recently in a remote cottage with a glorious view of Loch Ewe and the mountains beyond. I've tramped over that landscape, been awestruck by the views in all kinds of weather, sat cosy inside and watched sheets of rain move across the hills. So the pictures in my head were vivid and clear.

However, the real jumping-off point for the story happened not there but in Cromarty, on the Black Isle on the opposite coast. I'd popped into the local bookshop to see whether they had anything about the Highlands during the Second World War. I was out of luck on that score, but the bookseller told me an extraordinary anecdote about a couple who had been in the shop recently. They'd been on an unsuccessful quest to uncover a wartime legacy.

But my mind immediately turned to the possibilities of a very different outcome. A dark and twisted outcome, inevitably …

Wester Ross, with its scattered communities and dramatic landscapes, suggested itself to me as a setting for my story. Transplanting Karen so far from her office in Gayfield Square would wrong-foot her and make different demands on her, I thought. And I wanted to get away from the

RIGHT: The sort of road that leads to Hamish's croft.

PREVIOUS SPREAD: The mountains of Wester Ross from Loch Gairloch.

tartan and shortbread image many people have of the Highlands. Here's a conversation between local crofter Hamish Mackenzie and a couple of visitors from down south.

> Hamish chuckled. 'I hate to disillusion you, Alice, but [the landscape is] only timeless if you measure time in a relatively short span. People think of the Highlands as a wilderness. A kind of playground for people who want to go hunting, shooting, fishing and hiking. But it's as much a man-made environment as the big cities you leave behind you.'
>
> 'What do you mean?' Alice paused and looked around her at the heather and the hills, the rocky outcroppings pushing through the soil, their surfaces stained with lichen and moss. 'This looks pretty natural to me.'
>
> 'And that's because nature's had time to reclaim what we'd previously colonised. Go back three hundred years or so, and this glen would have been busy with people working the land. Just picture it. Smoke rising from somewhere between a dozen and twenty chimneys. A few cattle here and there on the common grazing. Crops growing in run rigs, every croft farming its own five acres.' Hamish pointed towards the sparkle of the sea loch beyond the margin of the machair. 'Down on the shore, a few small boats, their fishing nets spread out for drying and mending.'

Karen does appreciate the scenery and its nuances, but she doesn't fall into the trap of easy sentimentality either.

Looking south from the shores of Loch Thurnaig, Wester Ross.

Loch Ewe in Wester
Ross, a major naval
base in the Second
World War.

They walked into a bright half-moon-shaped room, with big triple-glazed windows round the outside walls. The uninterrupted view was even more spectacular than from the road. Being so close to the sea made Karen feel instantly at home, although this prospect of water and mountains was on a far grander scale than the view of the Firth of Forth and Fife from her flat. *I could live here.* Then reason kicked in and she realised she'd never survive without her friends, her family, her job. The streets she walked at night. You couldn't outrun what lived inside you; you could only make accommodation with it. And for her, running away would never be the answer.

One of the joys of playing god in my own universe is the chance to tip my hat to places I know and love. I've been a visiting tutor at Moniack Mhor, Scotland's Creative Writing Centre, since it opened back in the 1990s. Every couple of years, I take a week out of my schedule to work with emerging writers. It's the only time in my writing life that I actually talk about craft and there's a real buzz from working intensely with beginning writers who are passionate about what they're attempting. Moniack is an inspiring place, high on a plateau surrounded by mountains and forest. And yet it's less than half an hour from Inverness. I love it there, so I stole its setting for a small episode in *Broken Ground*. I hope it is a memory-jogger for anyone who's been to Moniack.

> There were places in Scotland where satnav was as much use as a chocolate compass. Wester Fearn House was one of them. It was nominally part of a hamlet called Teavarran, which the officious woman who lived in the car's computer believed she'd brought them to. But it wasn't really a place, just a road through a wood that opened out on to high moorland. They passed a beautifully renovated stone house and a writers' centre before Karen was able to make sense of the map.

A few years ago, I was surprised to be invited to be Chieftain of the Invercharron Highland Games. Of course, I accepted, because new experience is food and drink to a writer. We had beautiful weather for our drive up to the games grounds just outside Bonar Bridge on the eastern side of Sutherland. The field of combat sits between heather-covered hills and the sparkling water of the Kyle of Sutherland. My first task was to march round the running track at the head of the pipe band with a targe – a large shield – and a sword. Then I had to smite the targe with the sword to signal the start of the games.

It was a day full of impressive achievements. A fell race to the top of the hill and down again; bagpipe competitions; Highland dancing contests; tug of war; track and field athletic events; and for me, the jewel in the crown: the heavy athletes. These are the strongmen who toss cabers, throw hammers, fling stones and, most terrifyingly impressive to me, perform the Weight for Height event. This is how I describe it in *Broken Ground*:

> A hush always shivered through the crowd when it came to the most terrifying event of the games. He would make great play of rubbing his palms with the rosin bag to protect him from the nightmare injuries that slippage could cause. He would check the height the bar was set at, then he'd turn his back on the two slender uprights and the crossbar. He'd plant his feet firmly apart then bend his

Throwing the Weight for Height.

knees, taking a firm grasp of the 56lb weight with one hand. Then he'd swing it back and forth, up and down, to build momentum, his kilt swaying dramatically with each smooth movement. Three times, and then he would release the block of iron with a prayer.

If it went well – and so far, for him, it had always gone well – the weight would sail up over his head and high into the air. The crowd would gasp, the lump of iron would seem to freeze at the apex of its climb then it would descend on the far side of the bar, not even causing it to tremble. And then the crowd would roar. The world record stood an inch over nineteen feet. He was three inches behind.

Sometimes it did not go well and the bar came tumbling to the ground. And sometimes it went very badly indeed. Men had died on the field in front of families no longer having a good day out. But he refused even to consider that as a possibility. He threw with absolute faith in his command of 56lb of iron as aerodynamic as a breezeblock.

We held our breath every time one of the heavily muscled men grasped the ring on top of the iron block. Thankfully, there were no accidents. But I seized the chance to talk to some of the competitors. And what I learned found its way into this book. Because, to a writer, nothing is ever wasted.

Although the story in *Broken Ground* starts in the Highlands, it doesn't end there. Karen's travels take her to Elgin in Speyside where she wanders by the river at night; to cafés and restaurants in Edinburgh, some real, others fictitious; and to the First Minister's official residence, Bute House in Charlotte Square in Edinburgh. Her colleagues explore other places that also reflect modern Scotland – the picture-postcard prettiness of Portpatrick in the far south-west; the blighted town centre

of Motherwell that only a mother could love; the campus of Stirling University, designed to share its plate glass and concrete with nature in a forced harmony that sometimes works.

That's part of the excitement of living in Scotland. It may be a small country but its people and its places are varied. All my life, it's surprised me. Sometimes with delight and sometimes with despair. But always with a provocation to think and feel. And because I'm a writer, to attempt to capture something of it in words. Fortunately, the camera exists to fill in my failures.

The notorious chandelier in the drawing room of Bute House.

And finally …

A few years ago I was invited by the Jura Distillery to come for a visit. We were there for eight days, a period which included three ceilidhs and one regatta. Not bad for an island whose population in the last census was less than two hundred. As well as knowing how to have a good time, they also know how to make very good whisky. In return for their generosity, I wrote a short story which isn't readily available. As a final treat for this journey round my Scotland, here is that story.

LEFT: Evans Walk, a stalkers' path on Jura.

ABOVE: The Jura whisky distillery.

SIXTEEN

THE DEVIL'S SHARE

The rocks were slippery with spray from the high waterfall. The brown water, broken white by the height of the cascade, gleamed and glistened and glittered, the same colour as the whisky that emerges from the other end of the distilling process. The three youngsters clambered hesitantly up the steep hillside, stopping frequently to catch their breath. They were accustomed to being out of the city, to running wild through the landscape. But their usual landscape was tamer than the wildness of Jura. They'd learned their freedom on sand dunes and waymarked woodland paths, not this raw world of rock and heather, bracken and pines, sudden flows and pools of water. Here, it was easy to lose any sense of direction. To a stranger, one stalking moor looks much like another. To a newcomer, all of the three breast-shaped Paps look the same. A recipe for disorientation.

Nervous of this, Jack kept checking over his shoulder to make sure of his bearings. He understood that being eldest meant he'd carry the blame if anything went sour. But so far, everything was sweet. He could see the slate roof of the four-square Georgian lodge next to the distillery and beyond that, the Bay of Small Isles, a couple of small yachts bobbing at anchor. At dinner the night before, they'd watched the boats sail in to the sheltered anchorage. He'd been glad they were staying in the lodge and not confined on a boat at the mercy of unpredictable weather and queasiness. Much better to be able to walk out the front door and feel solid ground under your feet.

And then the ground shifted beneath him. A yell, almost a scream, rose above the roar of the water. Jack whirled round, just in time to catch the final moment of Cameron's tumble from the rocks into the cascade. Jack's imagination leapt ahead and for a moment he couldn't work out why his cousin's body wasn't being tossed down the waterfall, at the mercy of the joint forces of water and gravity. But Cameron had apparently disappeared. The screaming Jack could hear now came from his sister Roisin, still clinging to the rocks but reacting as if she was the one in trouble.

PREVIOUS SPREAD: The ferry from Islay to Jura, with the Paps of Jura happed in mist.

Jack carefully picked his way back down to his sister's side and shouted, 'Where's Cameron?'

She stopped screaming long enough to give him a look of contemptuous dismissal. 'He's in the waterfall.'

'How can he be *in* the waterfall?'

She shrugged. 'I don't know. But he fell in and he didn't come out so he must still be in there, right? I mean, it's not like it's a portal to another dimension, is it?'

Jack looked at the tumbling water. For all he could see of his cousin, Roisin's sarcasm could have hit the mark. He stared intently into the water, willing Cameron to appear. When he saw a flicker of red, he wondered momentarily whether he'd wished it into being. Then he saw it again, and this time he was sure it was Cameron's T-shirt. 'Look, there he is,' he cried. 'There must be a ledge or a cave or something. Roisin, go back down for help.'

For once, she didn't need telling twice. Jack watched her scrambling descent, willing her not to fall and double his problems. Once she disappeared, cut off from him by the distillery buildings and the lodge below, he turned back to the waterfall. Yes, he could definitely catch glimpses of the shirt. And it looked like Cameron was moving around, so he absolutely wasn't dead or seriously injured. Jack settled on a rock to wait, arms curled round his bent legs, his body folded tight against itself, holding in the fear.

The rescue seemed to take no time at all. Within minutes of Roisin disappearing, bodies had emerged on the hillside, swarming up the rocks, sure-footed and serious, bred-in-the-bone Diurachs and incomers both. Nicol the boatman reassured Jack with a friendly arm round his shoulders while others roped themselves into a human chain and moved into the turbulent water. Their approach was cautious without being tentative and sooner than seemed possible, they were backing out of the broken wall of water with Cameron's skinny body clamped round the leader like a baby spider monkey.

With perfect timing, the mothers arrived. The burly man who had led the rescue peeled Cameron off and passed him to his mother. She hugged him close, both shivering with shock and relief. Past fear now, he loosened his grip and half-turned towards the waterfall. 'There's a barrel of whisky in there,' he said.

The Diurachs exchanged doubtful looks then turned their faces towards Willie Cochrane, the Glaswegian distillery manager. He shook his head. 'That cannae be right. We can account for every cask. Customs and Excise make sure of that.'

Cameron's smile was conciliatory. 'No, really. Honestly. There's a barrel just like the ones you showed us in the warehouse.'

'There's only one way to find out,' Nicol said, looking expectantly at the rescuers.

The leader shrugged. 'Why not? We're already wet. Anybody got a light?'

One lad had a rubber-encased torch clipped to his belt. He handed it over without a word and the men stepped back under the battering shower of the waterfall.

While the mothers fussed over Cameron, everyone else milled around making a meal of doing nothing useful. They didn't have long to wait. The men emerged, backing out of the water and shaking themselves like dogs. 'The boy's right,' the leader said. 'I've no bloody idea how they got it up there, but there's a wee cave in the rocks, hardly room to stand up in. And right at the back, there's a whisky barrel.'

'That cannae be,' Willie repeated, shaking his head vigorously. 'No way.'

'It's no' your problem, Willie,' the man said. 'It's a 1901 cask.'

Incredulity widened Willie's eyes. A broad grin spread across his small features. 'You're kidding me.'

'I'm telling you. It must have been one of the last casks out of the old distillery before they closed it down.'

Willie rubbed his hands. A 111-year-old whisky; he could see the pound signs already. 'So, how do we get it out of there?' he said.

Archie Maclean liked to sit by the window. His cottage was tucked away at the end of a track, the best thing about it the view of the raised beach above Loch Tarbert. Mostly the only sounds were the sea and the birds, except when the choppers came clattering in with VIP guests ferried up for a bit of stalking and shooting on Lord Astor's estate. That was one of the few things that had changed in this corner of the island since he was a boy. Ninety-two now, with plenty of aches and pains to prove it. But he didn't feel close to death.

Jura had a tradition of longevity. Some scientist had told them it was something to do with high levels of selenium in the water. Archie thought it was most likely because of clean air, hard but simple living and decent whisky. For years, they'd had to rely on friends and family across the narrow strait on Islay for a reliable supply of a good dram, but since the distillery had started up again forty years before, there had been no shortage among the locals.

He checked his watch. In ten minutes, he'd turn the radio on to catch the national news. Getting old didn't mean you had to give up on understanding the world. Once a week, his great-grandson Callum took him down to the Service Point at Craighouse where he could use the internet to email his son in New Zealand and his daughter in Spain. Archie liked to browse the web too, following links into strange nooks and crannies of cyberspace.

A couple of guillemots caught his eye and he followed their flight across the loch and out of sight. An unexpected sound made him cock his head to one side, straining to make it out. Then he relaxed. Callum's Land Rover, its clapped-out diesel engine coughing up the track. Archie smiled and pushed up on the arms of his chair, creaking to his feet and heading for the kitchen. He liked that Callum stopped in for these unscheduled visits. Archie didn't want his family to come by out of obligation. He'd rather be on his own than feel like a charitable deed. But he'd always had a special bond with Callum, the eldest of his generation.

The engine cleared its throat and died away. Archie felt the cool air of the afternoon as the door opened and Callum strode in. He gave Archie's thin shoulders a squeeze on his way to one of the kitchen chairs.

'Your hair's wet,' Archie said.

'Nothing gets past you, Daddo. You'll never believe what we've been up to.' Callum shook his big head, the shaggy reddish hair falling in damp locks to his shoulders.

'Try me.' Archie put teabags in mugs and poured boiling water on them.

'You know the river that comes down from the Market Loch?'

'The whisky river?' Archie stirred the brew and carefully lifted the bags out, laying them on a saucer he left by the kettle for that purpose.

'Aye. Well, one of the bairns on holiday at the lodge fell into the waterfall this morning, so we had to go in after him. Because he'd disappeared. Like magic.'

Startled, Archie slopped tea on the table. Callum jumped up and fetched a cloth, cleaning the spillage while the older man groped for a chair and sat heavily. 'A cave?' His voice was weak and querulous.

'Aye, a cave. Good guess, Daddo.'

'Ach, that hillside's got a fair few caves dotted about. It's no' rocket science.'

'So, it's a cave. We get the bairn out, no bother. But he starts going on about a cask of whisky in the cave. Willie was there, and he was adamant it couldnae be one of his. But the bairn was just as adamant about what he'd seen. So, more to humour him than anything else, we went back in. And right enough, there was a barrel.'

Archie sipped his tea hoping it would ease the nausea churning his stomach. 'That's amazing,' he said, sounding anything but amazed.

'But Willie was right, it wasnae one of his barrels. Guess what it was?'

'I don't know.' Archie stared into his tea. 'From Islay?' It was a reasonable guess – at any given time over the past century there had been at least half a dozen distilleries on the island across the narrow strait from Jura.

'Better than that. It's a 1901 barrel from the old Jura distillery itself. Willie was about passing out with the excitement.'

'Aye? I bet he was.'

Callum took a healthy swig of tea. 'Christ knows how they got it up there in the first place.'

'They'll never get it down again, surely?' Archie sounded nonchalant, but his lumpy arthritic fingers clutched his mug close to his chest.

Callum tapped the side of his nose. 'Know-how, that's what it takes. Norman Shaw had the very thing on the boat. A big tripod for a block and tackle. The lads lashed the barrel with ropes and guided it out through the rocks, then Norman let it down the slope bit by bit. We had one or two hairy moments, but nobody got hurt and neither did the barrel. Amazing sight, Daddo. You could still make out the writing on the barrel end – "Jura 1901".'

'So where's the barrel now?'

'Willie and his crew huckled it away into the bond. I mean, technically it doesn't belong to the distillery, but nobody wants to get into a *Whisky Galore* scenario with the exciseman. The bond seemed like the best solution. Willie's going to broach the cask tomorrow and see what the whisky is like. If it's any good at all, he'll get the master blender over from the mainland. See, if it's special, Willie says it'll be sold for a lot of money and we'll all get a cut. Once Robert Paterson's given it the stamp of approval, the sky's the limit.'

Archie stared over Callum's shoulder at the corner of Loch Tarbert visible through the kitchen window. 'I've got a feeling it'll be special, all right.'

Callum finished his tea and stood up. 'I hope so. I could do with a few bob. Get some work done on the Land Rover. And maybe a new outboard for the dinghy.' He patted Archie on the shoulder. 'I'll see you on Thursday, Daddo. Usual time, eh?' Lost in his dreams of engines, he didn't notice Archie's failure to say farewell.

What would a body look like after sixty-four years steeped in whisky in an oak cask? Archie had once found a forensic anthropology forum where some American professor answered people's questions. Some of the things they wanted to know were worryingly bizarre. 'What would a pubic scalp in a jar of formalin look like?' one had wanted to know. 'Tinned tuna, with hair,' had been the laconic response.

He'd come back a couple of weeks later and asked, 'What would a body look like if it had been in a barrel of whisky for fifty years?'

The answer had appeared almost immediately.

'Your body would be perfectly preserved, provided he was completely covered by the alcohol,' the professor had written. 'Everything would be as is, inside and outside the body. You'd even have the stomach contents perfectly preserved so you could tell what he ate for his last meal fifty years before. There would only be one major change. Just as whiskey gets its colour from the wood it's matured in, so your guy would have taken on the same colouration. If he started out a white man, he's going to be pretty damn dark after fifty years. Even the whites of his eyes will have changed colour – he's going to look jaundiced at the very least.'

It wasn't the answer he'd expected. He'd thought the whisky would be more like acid, slowly eating the body away. He'd been convinced that after all this time, there would be nothing left of Jock Lindsay except some sediment at the bottom of the barrel. The notion that he was hanging there, suspended like a museum specimen, was unsettling. Still, Archie had told himself, the cave and its secret had been undisturbed for more than half a century. The chances were it would stay that way until he was long gone. These days, he doubted there was anyone else left who could put a name to the dead man.

Archie washed the mugs and set them on the drainer. There was another helping of his grand-daughter's venison casserole in the fridge. He'd been planning on having it with a few potatoes and carrots for his tea. But he wasn't in the mood. Instead, he filled his battered hip flask with sixteen-year-old Jura, put on his old tweed stalking jacket and headed out the door, leaning heavily on his walking stick.

He took his time walking down to the raised beach, where he settled on his usual flat-topped boulder. These days, there was no padding on his bony backside and he knew he wouldn't be able to sit for long. At least the midges had given up on him. Nothing left to suck out of him, he often thought. Archie unscrewed his flask and sipped at the warm peaty drink. He could feel the heat all the way down to his stomach. 'Make the most of it,' he said out loud.

A faint breeze ruffled the inlet of the loch that lapped down below. From here, he could see a couple of the trig points that formed the ingenious navigation system set up in the 1960s to ease the treacherous passage up the snaking waterway that led from the sea to the Loch Tarbert anchorage. Before that, the rocky shallows had ripped the bottom out of plenty of strangers' boats. And a few locals who'd grown too cocksure as well.

Back in 1948 there had been no trig points. Just a couple of painted rocks to show the way. It had been a simple job to cover the painted rocks with sacks and paint a couple of decoys. Archie had known that would be enough to confound Jock Lindsay. Although Jock had grown up on Jura he'd cleaved to the land, not the sea. He might have managed to steer his boat up the loch if everything had been where it was supposed to be, but Archie had put paid to that. The motorbike Jock had been carrying on board had made certain his boat would sink as soon as it was holed. Struggling to shore in the dark, weighed down by heavy boots and clothes, Jock had been no match for Archie. Archie had known he'd need every ounce of that advantage; Jock was bigger and tougher and more ruthless than he'd ever been. But he'd been determined to stop Jock. And if that meant stooping to dirty tricks, so be it.

It had ended in murder but it had begun in the schoolroom. Archie and Jock had attended the village school together and when war had broken out, they'd enlisted together, both joining the Parachute Regiment. They'd both had the kind of war that makes a man glad to be alive and whole. Archie knew Jock had seen and done worse than he'd had to deal with. That meant it had been very bad indeed.

After the war, Jock had stayed on in the Army, but Archie had been desperately grateful to return to Jura. He'd found work on the Ardlussa estate in the north of the island, turning his hand to whatever was needed. When the Fletchers had let Barnhill to Eric Blair, the writer the world knew as George Orwell, he'd been told to do what he could to help out but to make it as discreet as possible. He'd done his best, and although Mr Blair's sister had a tongue on her that would strip paint if she was crossed, Archie kept his head down and tried to stay invisible when Mr Blair was up and about.

But mostly, the writer did what writers do. He stayed in his room and hammered away on a typewriter. Sometimes when Archie was crossing the garden, he could hear the clatter of the keys punctuated by the wee tinkle of the carriage return bell, then a salvo of coughing would interrupt the process.

Archie had never been much of a reader but he knew that Mr Blair's books were supposed to be important. He was all for the working man, apparently, though Archie never managed to have any kind of conversation with him. He'd written some book where the animals took over, but it wasn't really about the animals, it was about Communism. It had sold a lot of copies, according to Mrs Fletcher down at the big house.

Miss Blair said the book her brother was writing now would be even more remarkable. She was a wee bit vague on the details, but she did say it would be very political and it would make a lot of people very angry. 'Especially the silly beggars who think that just because the Russians were on our side during the war that they're the sort of people we want to have as allies now it's all over,' she'd said primly one afternoon when they'd been earthing up the potatoes.

Everything had been going fine for Archie. The work at Ardlussa and Barnhill was hard, but he'd got the tenancy of a decent cottage, he'd married Morna Stewart and their first child was on the way. And then he'd had a postcard from Jock Lindsay.

'I'm coming home on leave. See if you can get to Craighouse on Saturday, we'll have a drink.'

Archie wasn't bothered about going drinking with Jock Lindsay. He could think of better ways to spend his money. But Morna picked up the card and nudged him. 'Go on, Archie. You work hard, you deserve a wee bit of fun.'

'I get plenty of fun with you.'

She giggled. 'There's more to life than an Inverlussa ceilidh. Speak to Mrs Fletcher. I'm sure there'll be something needing taking down on the lorry to Craighouse. Or fetching back.'

And so he'd gone.

They'd had a couple of pints in the bar, then Jock had led Archie out on to the pier, producing a flat half-bottle from inside his battledress. He pulled out the cork and passed the bottle to Archie. 'Help yourself,' he urged. 'It's the good stuff from Islay.'

Archie took a tentative sip. The phenolic taint of heavily peated, oily spirit filled his mouth, clearing out his sinuses and making his head swim. 'Christ, Jock, that's some dram,' he said.

'Contacts, Archie. Contacts.'

They walked in silence to the end of the pier, passing the bottle back and forth between them. Finally, Jock turned to face Archie and said, 'So you're working for George Orwell.'

'We call him by his real name. Eric Blair. But aye, that's the way of it.'

'The people I work for, they don't think much of your Mr Blair.'

'Is that right? And who do you work for, Jock? I thought you were a soldier?'

'I am, Archie. But things are not as simple as they were when you wore the uniform. Back then, the enemy was obvious. Now, sometimes the enemy's well hidden.'

'How is Mr Blair anybody's enemy? He just writes books.'

Jock chuckled, a low menacing sound. 'Books that change people's minds, Archie. Books that twist the truth and tell lies. Your Mr Blair, he talks about being for the working man. He claims he's a socialist. But his last book made a mockery of socialism. It made the working man look like a fool. And the word is that he's writing a book now that will turn people away from the left. And where does that leave us? It leaves us puppets of America, that's what. The only thing that will keep us safe is the balance of power, and if we turn our face away from Russia, then we've thrown in the towel. We've traded our sovereignty for Uncle Sam's bribery.'

Archie shook his head, bewildered. He'd never heard Jock talk like this. Nobody from here talked like this. 'Balance of power.' 'Sovereignty.' 'Uncle Sam's bribery.' That was the kind of thing politicians talked about on the radio, not what your pals talked about on a Saturday night out.

'You've grown awfu' political,' he said.

'The people I work for, they've shown me how the world works, Archie.'

Archie scratched his chin. 'Is that right?'

'Archie, you know me. We've been in tight corners together. You know you can trust me.' Jock sounded confident, nudging Archie's arm as he passed the bottle.

'Trust you how?'

'I've got a mission,' Jock said. 'Orders from on high. They don't want your Mr Blair's new book to see the light of day. I hear he's very ill?'

Reluctantly, Archie nodded. 'Aye. There's nothing of him. I sometimes think another winter will see him off. But he's a tough old bird. You never know with his kind.'

Jock took out a pack of cigarettes and offered one to Archie, who shook his head. He'd never taken to tobacco, something he was glad of when he heard Mr Blair's racking cough echo across the garden. A real smoker's cough, that was. Jock lit his own fag then said, 'I've been ordered to destroy the manuscript of this new book. Whatever it takes.'

The words lay between them like a stone. Archie didn't know anything about books but he knew plenty about hard work. And he understood the physical cost to Mr Blair of writing the book that, according to his sister, was close to being finished. 'Is that why you're here?'

Jock laughed. 'No. I'm here because I need help from an old comrade in arms. When I come back, I'll need someone who knows the lie of the land to get me into Barnhill without raising the alarm. In and out, nobody any the wiser. And a good job done without any bother. That's where you come in, Archie.'

Archie shook his head. 'I can't do that. They've been very decent to me.'

Jock suddenly gripped his arm. 'This isn't about you, Archie. This is for your country. Your patriotic duty. See this uniform? It's the same one we both wore to fight the Nazis. These battles now, they're just as important. If you don't help me, it's a kind of treason, Archie.'

Put like that, it was hard to argue against. Jock had always had a forceful personality. By the end of the half-bottle, they'd agreed on the date. Jock, ever confident, said he'd bring a boat up Loch Tarbert. After all, it was the only anchorage on the island that was sheltered from passing boats or road vehicles. Jock would have a motorbike on board. He'd pick up Archie, who would ride pillion. They'd drive as near as they dared to Barnhill, then Archie would lead Jock to the farmhouse. 'I'll take you to the foot of the stairs and no further,' Archie had said. It was the one point on which he wouldn't give way.

But Jock had been relaxed about it. Now he saw the way clear to his objective, he was restored to his usual expansive self. Archie hid his unease but it was still there, burning and grumbling in his stomach like a bad pint.

In the morning, driving back to Ardlussa, squinting against the dull headache the drink had left in its wake, Archie pondered what Jock had told him. The more he thought about it, the more naïve he felt. Jock had sold him a tale about destroying a manuscript. But that was pointless while the author of that manuscript still lived. And he knew Jock well enough to believe he'd never leave a job half-done. That 'whatever it takes' of Jock's had been sufficiently explicit to men who'd been through what they'd seen and done in the war.

It wouldn't be hard to kill Eric Blair, a man weakened and diminished by his illness. A pillow over his face, his body pinned by Jock's superior weight, and it would all be over in minutes. No struggle to wake the house. Nobody would think twice about it, given how ill Mr Blair had been. And the manuscript burned in the fireplace – the act of a man who knew himself to be at death's door, a man dissatisfied with the quality of his work. That was a scenario that made a lot more sense than Jock's nonchalant destruction of a manuscript.

Archie knew he couldn't live with such an outcome. Jock might claim his bosses were patriots, but this wasn't a patriotism Archie recognised. It wasn't what he'd fought for.

And so he made his choice.

What to do with Jock's body was the only thing that made him fret. He didn't want to leave it to the sea loch because it would eventually turn up somewhere. No, let Jock's paymasters wonder what had gone wrong. If they couldn't figure that out, it might keep them from trying again.

It was a problem that nagged him for days. He knew from his wartime experiences that bodies had a way of reappearing. He didn't want that to happen with Jock. He didn't want that hanging over his daily life. He wanted Jock out of sight and out of mind permanently. Archie dug potatoes and staked beans, gralloched deer and rowed out in the insect-thick dusk to fish, but always, he was worrying away at the problem. Soon he would run out of time.

Ironically, it was Mr Blair himself who gave him the key. Archie had been shifting boulders all day, trying to reshape a field so it would be easier to plough. Blair had walked down from the house towards the end of the afternoon. 'If you'd like a brandy when you're finished, come up to the house. It's all we've got, I'm afraid. If we still had a distillery on the island, I'd be able to offer you a whisky,' he'd said.

And then Archie knew what to do with Jock Lindsay's body.

His father had been working at the old distillery when it had closed down in 1901. Angry locals had removed half a dozen casks from the bonded store and hauled them up into the caves on the hill above the distillery. Over time, the contents had been shared out among the workers. But somebody talked when they shouldn't have and Craighouse had a surprise visit from the exciseman. Archie's father and his pals had shifted the last remaining cask into a cave beside the waterfall. And then one of the idiots had tried to camouflage it further by shifting some of the rocks.

The resulting rock fall left the barrel more or less inaccessible. Over time, people forgot about it. There was enough contraband whisky making its way over from Islay for there to be no burning need for a cask of not very good Jura whisky, even if it was free.

So Archie borrowed one of the horses from Ardlussa and headed down to Craighouse with a sack of potatoes to sell. Late that evening, he found a way through the water to the cave. The cask was still there, damp but unbroached. He'd brought hammer and chisel so he could remove the barrel end. By the light of a torch held in his teeth, he prised open the oak cask, almost knocked back on his heels by the pungent wave of peaty spirit when the wooden disc came free. The cask was still almost full, having lost only a small percentage of its contents to natural evaporation. The angels' share, the distillers called it. Jock would displace a serious amount of whisky, but there would be enough left to submerge him once Archie had rammed him inside.

Four days later, Archie proved his hypothesis. Carrying Jock up the steep hillside had nearly killed him, but fear of the hangman's rope had spurred him on. It was, after all, no different from carrying wounded comrades back to the medics. Easier, in fact, because there was no fear of enemy snipers or mines underfoot.

The struggle to get them both into the cave was risky and terrifying, but Archie was determined. He slid the body into the cask and pushed down, soaking himself in the pungent malt whisky up to the armpits. The whisky sloshed around his feet, disappearing quickly into the earthen floor of the cave. Jock seemed to fold like a concertina into the cask, his back and knees wedging him tight into the staves. And yes, there was plenty of whisky to cover him. The cask was full to the brim again.

Archie dropped the lid back in place. He'd helped himself to a tube of RTV sealant from the boathouse at Ardlussa and he carefully squeezed the compound into the gaps he'd chiselled out of the lid to free it from the staves. When he'd done, he ran his thumb over the joints, making sure they were properly sealed. Then he moved to the very edge of the cave and let the water thunder down over him. It was like being struck by a hundred hands, but he knew it would cleanse him of the whisky. And of any blood that had leaked from Jock's head wound.

Afterwards, that he seemed to be able to put the whole business out of his mind shocked Archie. But it was true. When he remembered that night, it always came as a surprise. Almost as if it had happened to someone else. He didn't live in constant fear of the cask being discovered. He didn't shy away from speculation about what Jock Lindsay might be up to these days. He didn't wake in the night hearing the iron bar smash Jock's skull with a sound like a melon hitting a stone floor.

He didn't even take particular pride in the success of *Nineteen Eighty-Four*, Mr Blair's acclaimed novel. Never even read it. Archie just got on with his life, a well-respected member of the community. A decent husband, father, grandfather and great-grandfather. If anyone had thought to ask, his family would have said he'd had a pretty uneventful life.

And now all that was about to end. Somewhere down the line, some smart forensic scientist would identify Jock Lindsay. Military records would tie him to Archie and there would be a knock at the door. Archie didn't have it in him to lie, not confronted with a direct question. At least Morna was long away to a place where his past couldn't hurt her.

On Thursday, when Callum's Land Rover drew up at the cottage, Archie was already at the door, breathing in the familiar air. But Callum was too full of his own news to register surprise. As soon as he was within hailing distance, he said, 'You'll never guess what's happened! Willie Cochrane hammered a spigot into the whisky cask they found in the waterfall. But there was more than whisky in the barrel – there was a body. A man with his head smashed in. Can you believe it?' He spread his arms in an expansive gesture of amazement.

'I know,' Archie said.

'Did somebody phone you and tell you?' Callum looked disappointed. Then he brightened up. 'Willie said, "at least they didn't spoil a cask of the good stuff". Because apparently, the old distillery malt wasnae up to much.'

Archie nodded. 'So I've heard. I wonder, Callum, could we go some place different today?'

Callum frowned. 'Not the Service Point? How not? Where do you want to go?'

'We'll need to go across to Islay. To the police station. There's something I need to tell them.'

Bibliography

Report for Murder (The Women's Press, 1987)

Common Murder (The Women's Press, 1989)

Final Edition (The Women's Press, 1991)

The Mermaids Singing (HarperCollins, 1995)

Blue Genes (HarperCollins, 1996)

The Wire in the Blood (HarperCollins, 1997)

Killing the Shadows (HarperCollins, 2000)

The Last Temptation (HarperCollins, 2002)

The Distant Echo (HarperCollins, 2003)

Hostage to Murder (HarperCollins, 2003)

The Torment of Others (HarperCollins, 2004)

'The Writing on the Wall', from *Stranded* (Flambard Press, 2005)

The Grave Tattoo (HarperCollins, 2006)

A Darker Domain (HarperCollins, 2004)

Trick of the Dark (Little, Brown, 2010)

Northanger Abbey (The Borough Press, 2014)

The Skeleton Road (Little, Brown, 2014)

Splinter the Silence (Little, Brown, 2015)

Out of Bounds (Little, Brown, 2016)

'Ancient and Modern', from *Bloody Scotland* (Historic Environment Scotland, 2017)

Broken Ground (Little, Brown, 2018)

Additional picture credits

© Courtesy of HES (Ian G. Lindsay Collection): 16

Illustration by Dee Campling: 22

Reprinted by permission of HarperCollins Publishers Ltd: 34, 42, 50, 64, 72, 88, 112

ALAN OLIVER/Alamy Stock Photo: 130

ABOVE: Jura Distillery barrels.

PREVIOUS SPREAD: Loch Tarbert, Jura.